TECHNIQUES IN AMERICAN FOLK DECORATION

by Jean Lipman

With Practical Instruction
by Eve Meulendyke

Dover Publications, Inc., New York

Published in Canada by General Publishing Company, Ltd., 30 Lesmill Road, Don Mills, Toronto,
Ontario.
Published in the United Kingdom by Constable
and Company, Ltd., 10 Orange Street, London WC 2.

This Dover edition, first published in 1972 under
the title *American Folk Decoration*, is an unabridged
republication of the work originally published by
Oxford University Press, New York, in 1951. The
present edition is published by special arrangement
with Oxford University Press.

International Standard Book Number: 0-486-22217-9
Library of Congress Catalog Card Number: 77-182096

Manufactured in the United States of America
Dover Publications, Inc.
180 Varick Street
New York, N.Y. 10014

To S.L.M.

Acknowledgments

The idea for the publication was suggested by Morton Bartlett, director of *Bench and Brush,* as a result of a questionnaire that showed the need for a simple, practical survey of American folk decoration.

Oxford University Press endorsed the idea for the book, and Philip Vaudrin and John Begg carried out with enthusiasm and imagination all details of publication.

Volunteer editors, who contributed original material and read the text before publication, were Alice Winchester, editor of the magazine *Antiques;* J. W. McArthur, National Lead Company; Elliot Orr, professional restorer and decorator; and Nina Fletcher Little, Mary Allis, Clarence W. Brazer, and the late Hobe Erwin, authorities on early American decoration. Titus Geesey deserves special thanks for his constant help and for the scores of photographs he took for this book, not only for reproduction but to clarify such matters as the stylistic differences between New England and Pennsylvania tin.

The photo file of *Antiques,* the Index of American Design photographs and renderings, Carl Drepperd's Americana research file, color plates made for Mrs. C. Naaman Keyser's Home Craft Course booklets, and a color plate from Esther Stevens Brazer's *Early American Decoration* were most generously placed at our disposal. Many other institutions and individuals provided photographs of their material for reproduction.

Maryan Bowen, a member of the Brazer Guild of decorators and a professional decorator and teacher of early American decoration, did the page of practice brush-stroke painting reproduced in the chapter on tin, cut all the stencils that illustrate the stenciled decoration, and worked closely with the authors on the technical instruction published in the book. She has checked all the recommended methods with the standards of craftsmanship required by the Guild.

Louise Mazzuchelli made the map on pp. vi–vii and the line drawings that illustrate the text. We think these drawings are outstanding from the point of view of exact adherence to the original designs and maximum clarification of detail for the study and reproduction of folk decoration.

Connecticut
January 1951

J. L. and E. M.

Contents

GEOGRAPHY OF FOLK DECORATION

NEW YORK

- Rome
- Batavia
- Cooperstown
- Cortland
- Lisle
- Ithaca

PENNSYLVANIA

- Jonestown
- Wescoesville
- Millersburg
- Kutztown
- Reading
- Harrisburg
- Ephrata
- Lancaster
- Philadel[phia]
- Gettysburg

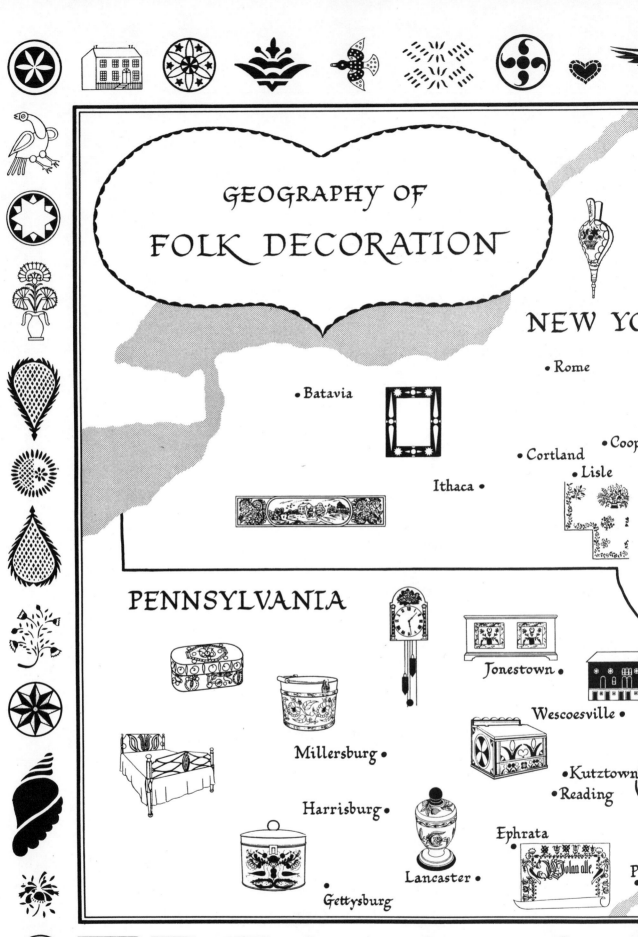

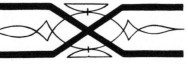

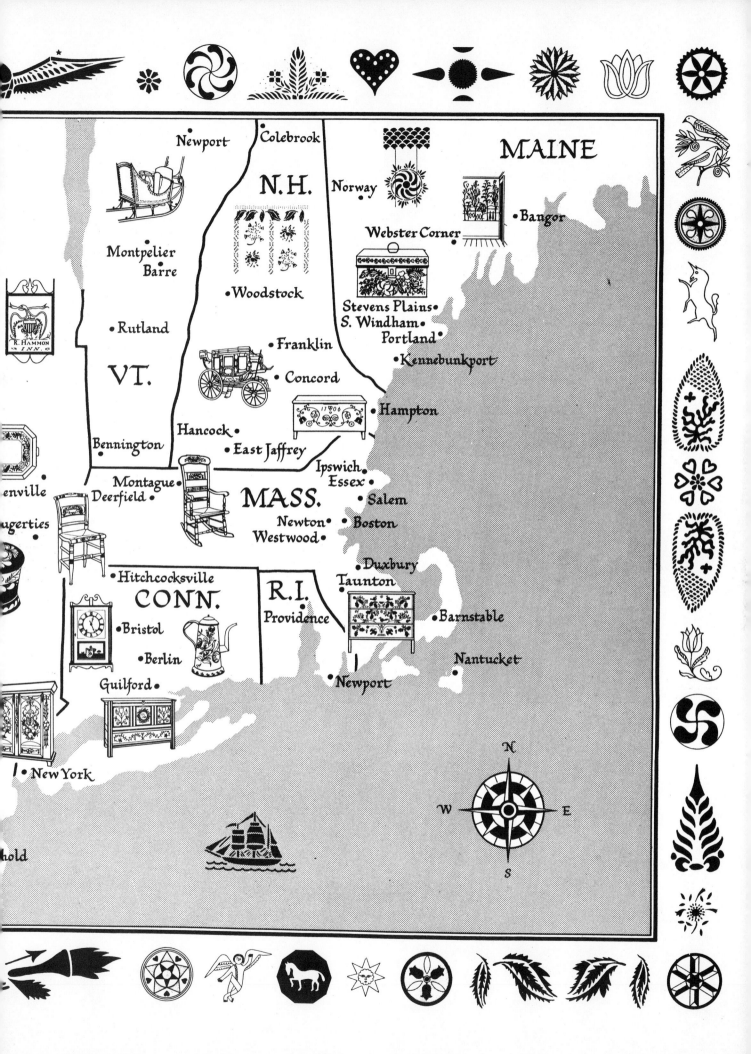

MAINE

Newport · Colebrook

N.H.

Norway

• Bangor

Webster Corner

Newport

Montpelier
Barre

Stevens Plains •
S. Windham •
Portland •

• Rutland

• Kennebunkport

• Woodstock

VT.

• Franklin

• Hampton

• Concord

Bennington

Hancock •

Montague •
Deerfield •

• East Jaffrey

Ipswich •
Essex •

enville

MASS.

• Salem

ugerties

Newton •
Westwood •

• Boston

• Hitchcocksville

CONN.

R.I.
Providence

• Duxbury
Taunton

• Bristol

• Berlin

Guilford •

• Barnstable

Nantucket •

• Newport

• New York

hold

N
W · E
S

List of Plate Illustrations

TIN

COACH AND SIGN PAINTING

PENNSYLVANIA FRACTUR
(watercolor and ink drawings)

American

Folk

Decoration

INTRODUCTION

Decorative Painting and the Painters

The painted decoration which is the subject of this book was executed by American craftsmen who worked mostly for middle-class country folk in the seventeenth, eighteenth, and nineteenth centuries. This homespun decorative painting which flourished in rural communities was quite different from the sophisticated and elaborate ornamentation fashionable in wealthy urban centers. The native decorators worked simply with an instinctive feeling for line and form and balance, producing a body of work that is distinguished by its stylized design and gay, strong color. This folk style in painted decoration is most attractive, suitable and easily reproduced for country homes today.

The chief kinds of American folk decoration are presented in seven chapters that deal with furniture, accessories, fabrics, tin, architectural decoration, coach and sign painting, and fractur. Each chapter is planned with a three-way approach to its subject.

The first part of the chapter is intended to give the reader a brief survey of the material under consideration, and to help the collector or decorator choose the most appropriate designs for his own type of home.

The text that follows is devoted to techniques. This was planned to provide practical instruction for amateurs, and incidentally to clarify the methods used by the old-time decorators. The general directions are supplemented by detailed descriptions for the reproduction of sample pieces that are illustrated in the plates. The line drawings and stencils accompanying the instruction are intended to be enlarged for use as working patterns for the designs.

A group of plates follows the text in each chapter. The individual illustrations were chosen with the idea of showing the most interesting types of American folk design, from the point of view of the student and collector and the home decorator who wishes to reproduce or adapt the designs.

The territory in which the decorative painters worked from the seventeenth through the nineteenth centuries stretched from the Atlantic seaboard through the West and South, but the folk decoration with which we are concerned was concentrated largely in New England and Pennsylvania. These were the craft centers of America, and decorative painting grew out of craft traditions. The map on pp. vi & vii of the book indicates the territory in which various kinds of folk decoration were typically found.

As we have indicated throughout the book, folk designs came from a variety of sources, the most important being pottery and porcelain; woven, printed, and embroidered textiles; carved woodwork, and wallpaper.

It is interesting to find that the same designs developed regional characteristics in different parts of the country. Tulips, for instance, were painted differently in New England and in Pennsylvania; and the popular heart motif varied, too, the Pennsylvania hearts being much wider because they were originally designed geometrically on the basis of three overlapping circles. It is also important to observe that folk decoration brought over from Europe developed its own style in America. We see how an imported folk art like fractur gradually achieved a native [1] style in Pennsylvania, with bolder design and simpler color.

The colors in American folk decoration are what they are for specific reasons. Since the early decorators commonly made their own colors, the range of hues was limited by the materials at hand. Even when 'store paint' was available, the plain old colors based on natural pigments remained popular in rural areas.

Many of the decorators used the native yellow, gray, gray-green, and red earth clays to make paint. When red clay was not locally available, yellow clay was baked to give it the desired red color; and brick dust was also made into a reddish paint. Natural vegetable dyes were used, too. Green was made from skunk cabbage, wintergreen, the crushed berries of dogwood, and from other shrubs and herbs. Madder came from the plant of that name, whose root gave a deep red color. Boiled walnuts yielded a mahogany dye, and boiled chestnuts a buff color. Other browns and brownish yellows were extracted from the bark of trees such as the red oak and the hickory. As blue was obtained from the flowers of the indigo plant, and had to be imported from India, it was relatively more scarce, and we find less of it than the other primary colors in early decoration.

Similar color schemes and designs were often used in various kinds of decoration, for the early decorators frequently worked in several fields. We find decorators of Pennsylvania chests who also executed fractur; house and sign painters who stenciled walls and floors, painted woodwork, and decorated fireboards; and coach painters who painted floor cloths and frescoed walls, and even japanned tin.

It was the decorators themselves—their work methods, tools, colors, and designs—who were the determining factor in the native style of our folk decoration. They were its common denominator. A great many of the decorators were itinerants, traveling through the countryside to seek work. Their rapid work methods, their crude paints and the primitive tools they carried in their saddlebags—cat's-hair brushes for painting fractur, a turkey feather for marbling floors, a cork and a sponge for mottling chests, a leather comb for graining woodwork—influenced the character of the decoration they executed. The itinerants carried the country styles of painted decoration from house to house and from town to town. They were the popular disseminators of culture and world news and local gossip, a vital connecting link between the scattered villages of the early American countryside.

General Suggestions for Home Decoration

REPRODUCING FOLK DESIGNS

To reproduce folk designs it is highly important to realize that each period and place carried its own typical form of decoration. Stenciled patterns should not be selected for articles which by their construction are dated prior to the use of stencils in decoration. Similarly, wood and tin patterns were not interchangeable and should be reserved for their own purposes if one aims at true reproduction. A study of original pieces and some knowledge of their history will help the beginner to determine a suitable decoration so that his reproduction will be authentic and appropriate. Even when early designs are adapted

for modern use, it is more satisfactory to adhere strictly to the original patterns and colors.

Before removing paint from an old piece, examine carefully for any trace of old decoration that may be saved. Should there be any indication of a design, wash with soap and water or rub gently with denatured alcohol to remove dirt and shellac. Apply a thin coat of varnish to make the pattern easier to see. When it is dry, trace on frosted acetate material (Supersee or a similar material), dull side up, all parts of the design that can be seen. Use India ink and a crowquill pen for permanent record. Colors may be copied with transparent paints or indicated with colored crayons for a guide when the piece is redecorated or whenever the pattern is used. These materials may be obtained in artists' supply stores.

Collectors should be on the lookout for fine old decorated pieces that have been repainted. The late coats of paint can be removed safely by using diluted, slow-acting paint remover and applying it to only a small area at a time so that the worker may keep up with the action of the paint remover and not permit it to penetrate into the design he wants to preserve. The new paint may be removed, when sufficiently softened, by rubbing lightly with a piece of cloth and, where flecks may be a bit stubborn, by picking off with a piece of pointed or flattened wood, depending on the surface. When all the undesirable new coats of paint have been removed, the piece should be wiped with a cloth that has been dipped lightly in turpentine and, when dry, waxed. Titus Geesey, a well-known collector of Pennsylvania antiques, reports that he has in his collection several fine old pieces that he treated in this way. The miniature dough trough (Figs. 47 and 48), which had six coats of paint over the original decoration, including a coat of white enamel, is one. The decoration on this piece is all original, not having been retouched in any way.

Nina Little, an authority on early American decoration, suggests that if an original design on wood, tin, or plaster is uncovered, it will be well to leave it untouched, even if it is in fragmentary condition, until real experience has been gained in that branch of painting. Remnants of fine painted decoration should not be ruined by clumsy overpainting in the wrong medium and with the wrong methods, when the character of the original work could be preserved by more expert restoration.

MATERIALS YOU WILL NEED

Brushes

KINDS OF BRUSHES. For all background work and varnishing, use the best ox, fitch, or badger-hair varnish brush obtainable, in ½ to 2 inch width, depending on the size of the piece to be painted.

Use a square-tipped, red-sable showcard No. 6 brush, or a No. 3 quill brush for painting a

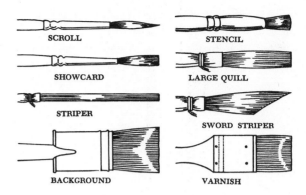

SCROLL   STENCIL

SHOWCARD   LARGE QUILL

STRIPER   SWORD STRIPER

BACKGROUND   VARNISH

design where details are 1 inch or more in width. This same-sized brush is used for applying color in bronze stenciling.

For smaller designs use quill brushes mounted on small sticks, in sizes No. 0-1 and 2 with hairs about ¾ of an inch long, and square-tipped.

The striping brush is an unmounted No. 1 quill brush with hairs 2 to 3 inches long. A fine dagger or sword brush may also be used for striping.

Scrolls and tendrils are made with No. 2 and No. 4 scroll brushes.

To stencil on fabric, use a No. 1 stencil brush.

For stenciling walls and floors you will usually need No. 2 and No. 4 stencil brushes. For painting walls and floors use brushes 3 to 4 inches wide.

For fractur work use small watercolor brushes.

CARE OF BRUSHES. Never allow a brush to dry with paint in it.

Suspend the varnish brush when not in use in a can of ½ turpentine and ½ linseed oil. Be sure the brush is free from turpentine and oil before using.

If the large brushes are not to be used again for a few days, clean first with turpentine, and then wash immediately by rubbing them on a cake of yellow soap and warm water until a heavy lather is formed. Rinse under running water and repeat until the brush is soft and free from paint. Brushes may also be cleaned with a liquid brush cleaner; follow directions on the container.

Small brushes should always be cleaned immediately with turpentine, kerosene, or cleaning fluid, or in a liquid brush cleaner.

A small bit of vaseline rubbed in the small brushes will keep them soft and pliable between use. Clean again before using. Wrap in wax paper for storage.

Paints

FOR WOOD OR TIN. For black backgrounds use flat black paint, which comes in cans already mixed. Thin with turpentine for free-flowing consistency.

For light- and medium-colored backgrounds use inside flat oil paint, either white or tinted, and tone with japan or artists' oil colors to the desired shade.

Japan colors or artists' oils are used for design painting and striping. Japan colors should be thinned with turpentine and a small bit of varnish added for free flowing. Artists' oils may be added to obtain desired color tone. With artists' oils use only varnish as a medium, never turpentine.

In using japan colors, it is well to squeeze the paint from the tube into a screw-top jar and cover with ¼ inch turpentine to keep from drying out. Small amounts of this may then be added to the flat paint to tone to the desired shade.

Artists' oil colors should be added direct from the tube.

In order to obtain a special color, it is possible to use japan paint for the background. Mix with turpentine to a creamy consistency and add a trace of varnish.

Keep some of the original paint in an air-tight container. You may need this for touching up after the decoration has been applied.

All background paints require at least 24 hours to dry between each coat. Although a flat paint may appear to be dry in less time, it softens when a second coat is applied too soon, leaving an uneven surface.

If, after the first coat of paint has thoroughly dried, brushy ridges should appear, sand them smooth and add more turpentine to your paint before applying a second coat.

FOR WALLS. Walls may be painted with either flat oil paint or casein water-mixed paint. Each has advantages. Your selection will depend upon your choice in regard to price, covering power,

speed of drying, ease of application, et cetera.

Both types of paint are available in a wide range of colors. If the colors your dealer has are not exactly what you want, he will gladly tell you which colors should be combined to obtain the desired result.

FOR WOODWORK AND FLOORS. Except in kitchens and bathrooms, where a high-gloss enamel is generally used, woodwork is painted with either flat oil paint or a semi-gloss enamel. The latter is preferred because it does not soil so easily and stands up better under repeated cleaning. Floor paint is used for floors. As with wall paints, enamels come in a wide range of colors. Many manufacturers make enamels in colors to match their flat oil paints.

FOR FABRICS. Textile colors are used.

FOR PAPER. Use pan, tube, or liquid watercolors.

Other materials needed for the preparation of surfaces and reproduction of designs are itemized in lists of required materials throughout the book.

HOW TO PREPARE WOOD FOR DECORATION

Old paint may be removed by scraping the surface with a hand scraper or by applying a paint remover. If a scraper is used, take care not to gouge the wood. Apply paint remover according to directions on the can. Wipe off, using No. 1 steel wool on the turnings. An orange stick or skewer will help get old paint out of the crevices.

When thoroughly cleaned down to the bare wood, the entire surface should be wiped with turpentine, Carbona, or denatured alcohol.

Let dry and then sand with a No. 4/0 garnet sandpaper, and No. 00 steel wool for the turnings.

Fill in holes with plastic wood, and sandpaper until smooth.

Old surfaces not requiring paint removal may be prepared by rubbing with powdered pumice and water mixed to a paste. New wood requires a coat or two of equal parts shellac and alcohol to seal the pores. Smooth with sandpaper when dry.

Materials	Where to buy	Amount
Scraper	Hardware store	1
Paint remover	Hardware store	1 can
Brush for paint remover	Hardware store	1
No. 1 steel wool	Hardware store	1 pk.
No. 00 steel wool	Hardware store	1 pk.
Orange stick	Drug store	1
Skewer	Dime store	1
Turpentine, Carbona, or alcohol	Hardware store	1 can
Shellac	Hardware store	1 pt.
Denatured alcohol	Hardware store	1 pt.
Powdered pumice	Drug store	3 oz.
Sandpaper No. 4/0 garnet	Hardware store	Several sheets
Plastic wood	Hardware store	1 tube

The preparation of fabrics, tin, and plaster for decoration is covered in chapters 3, 4, and 5.

HOW TO ENLARGE AND APPLY PATTERN TO SURFACE

To Enlarge Design

Trace the design on tracing paper and mark off with small squares over the design, numbering each square.

Take another piece of tracing paper the size of the panel or space to be decorated, and mark it off with the same number of squares, numbering each square to correspond with the numbers on the tracing.

Copy into each large square the exact detail found in the same numbered square on the smaller pattern.

It is possible, at small cost, to have a photostat made to enlarge or reduce the design to the proper size. Photostats of designs reproduced in books may be ordered by mail from any large library, such as the New York Public Library, by giving page reference to book and size of photostat desired. A price schedule, depending on size, will be sent on request by the photostatic department.

The actual size of each object reproduced in this book is given in the list of illustrations.

To Transfer Design

Trace design on thin tracing paper. Mark the exact center.

Rub back of tracing paper with a piece of magnesium carbonate. Fasten lightly to the space to be decorated with masking tape, centering the design. Trace with No. 3 pencil, and brush off excess chalk.

For light backgrounds, use black graphite paper under the tracing of your design.

Materials Required for Enlarging and Transferring Design

Materials	Where to buy	Amount
Tracing paper	Art supply store	1 pad
Magnesium carbonate	Drug store	1 cake
Black graphite paper	Art supply store	1 sheet
No. 3 pencil	Art supply store	1
Masking tape	Art supply store	1 roll
Ruler	Art supply store	1

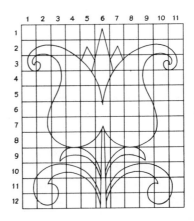

USE OF COLOR CHART AS GUIDE TO COLORING

The frontispiece color chart shows 12 old-time colors commonly used for early American decoration. All should be softened by antiquing with raw umber as described on p. 7.

The chart colors—tube oil and japan—are those used for decorating wood and tin. Textile paints, paints for walls and floors, and watercolors used for fractur are used in approximately the same shades.

To isolate one color on the chart in order to match it without distraction from the others, make a paper mask with one square cut out the size of the color squares. Place paper over chart, leaving uncovered only the square you wish to match.

FINISHING

Striping

Striping is usually used to frame the decoration, thus emphasizing the lines of construction. In planning the decoration of the piece, the purpose of this striping should be kept in mind to help to determine where it should be placed.

Since the background paint provides a dull surface, a better job results if a coat of varnish is applied first and allowed to dry for 24 hours. The varnish will avoid any possibility of the stripe drying with a fuzzy edge, and it has the additional advantage of making it possible to wipe off any errors in striping.

Various colors were used to stripe furniture and tin—fine vermilion stripes on light backgrounds, brown and black on green and yellow, white on red and gold, gold on black and white, et cetera. The most frequently used color combination was yellow on black. To mix this yellow use chrome yellow medium, toned to a mustard color with raw umber and a touch of yellow ochre.

Gold turnings and wide tray borders are done with a mixture of bronze powder and varnish.

Striping is usually done with japan paint softened in turpentine with a few drops of varnish added for smooth texture. Mix in a jar top or on a glass palette.

To stripe dip the striping brush (see p. 3) in the paint, full length. Test the consistency of the paint by pulling the brush across a piece of paper, drawing the brush toward you. If paint is thin, or pigment particles appear, clean brush and test again. Hold brush between the thumb and first two fingers, steadying it with the other fingers aganist the surface being striped. Always pull the brush toward you when striping a straight line.

When the paint seems evenly distributed in the brush, take a piece of paper and practice running a stripe along the edge about ⅛ of an inch from edge.

When you have practiced enough to give you confidence in your ability to run your brush evenly, you are ready to stripe the piece to be decorated. Should the line appear uneven, wipe off immediately and try again.

If the stripe is more than ½ inch from the edge, use a cardboard strip or ruler and a pencil to indicate the line. For a curved or irregular line, a pair of dividers may be used, one leg moving along the edge of the object while the other marks the parallel line.

Broad bands are more easily made with a double hairline stripe and then filled in with a hair showcard brush.

For curves or ovals, stripe is made clockwise. On curves, be sure to keep the tip of the brush in contact with the surface. Avoid using the broad side of the brush.

Varnishing

Do your varnishing on a clear day, with a room temperature of at least 70°. Never varnish on a rainy or hot, humid day, because the varnish will not dry.

Use great care to keep varnish free from dust. Keep the cover on the can at all times, and do not leave your brush lying in the open when not in use.

Work in a dust-free room. A bathroom previously filled with steam so that all dust particles are settled is an excellent place to do your varnishing.

Never dip your brush directly into the varnish can. Pour out a small amount in a saucer and keep the container covered.

Never shake the varnish can, since you may

stir up bubbles which will not settle for some time.

Use a ½ to 2 inch thin, flat varnish brush. Wipe out the first brushful by drawing it across a piece of paper. With the second brushful be sure the varnish is evenly distributed through the brush. Then apply a thin coat to the piece, using long, even strokes. A second stroking in the opposite direction is helpful.

Use a four-hour varnish, but allow to dry 24 hours, or more, between each coat, depending upon the drying conditions. Most surfaces require at least three coats of varnish.

If possible keep newly varnished work covered until dry, in order to prevent dust particles from settling on wet surfaces.

Antiquing

ANTIQUING ON WOOD WITHOUT A VARNISH COAT. For wood without a varnished finish, antique by rubbing the piece with a soft cloth dipped in raw linseed oil, mixed with a little turpentine and raw-umber tube color. Rub with clean cloth until practically dry. Repeat every few weeks until the desired effect is obtained. Destroy all oil rags after using them to prevent combustion.

ANTIQUING ON WOOD OR TIN WITH A LIGHT BACKGROUND THAT HAS HAD A VARNISH COAT. Add raw umber to a mixture of ½ turpentine and ½ varnish, and brush over the entire surface. Rub off after a few minutes with a clean, lintless cloth.

ANTIQUING ON WOOD OR TIN WITH A DARK BACKGROUND. Add a small amount of raw umber to the first coat of varnish. Allow to dry 24 hours. If you have not obtained the soft tone desired, again add a small amount of raw umber to the second coat of varnish. Use raw umber sparingly because too much added at one time will give a milky effect. The last two coats of varnish are always applied clear.

A final step in antiquing is to rub the object with powdered pumice and crude oil for a smooth finish, after the final coat of varnish has dried at least 48 hours.

ADVANCED INSTRUCTION

Specialized Books

Books giving advanced technical instruction in the various kinds of decoration may be studied and used. A number of these are listed in the Bibliography.

Decorating Lessons

Some of the decorating processes cannot be adequately mastered by the amateur without instruction from a professional. Teachers from local chapters of the Esther Stevens Brazer Guild of decorators are recommended. Many state adult-education extensions have qualified teachers.

CHAPTER 1

DECORATED FURNITURE

Types · Regions · Periods · Style · Decorators

Do you think of the typical early American home as plain, rather severe, and relatively colorless? It would not be surprising if you do, for though 'colonial' style has been very popular, architects, interior decorators, and department stores have tended to standardize and devitalize it by featuring natural pine for paneling, floors, furniture, and accessories; white painted exteriors, walls, and woodwork; and white curtains and bed canopies. Actually, from earliest times, the homes and furnishings of our ancestors were characterized by a wealth of vivid color and gay design.

The homestead was often painted Venetian red, russet, yellow ochre, or gray; when the house was white, the roof might be vermilion, the trim blue or green. Floors and woodwork were frequently painted pumpkin yellow, red, blue, or green, marbleized, stenciled in patterns, or finished in a variety of other ways. Plaster walls were often tinted gray, rose, or yellow, and a great many were adorned with painted landscapes or bright stenciled designs. Many early overmantel panels were decorated with landscapes, and the fireboards used to cover fireplaces during the summer were ornamented with landscape or still-life paintings. Fabrics were gay, too, and such things as stenciled bed covers, patterned carpets, and painted window shades added brisk color accents to the rooms. Accessories such as painted and stenciled boxes, picture frames, clocks, and mirrors further enlivened the decorative scheme.

The early decorated furniture, most of which has by now been ruthlessly scraped down and refinished, originally played a major part in the interior of the early American home. Furniture was most often painted in one or several colors, ornamented with painted designs, stenciled, japanned, or decorated with gold leaf or bronze paint. This old furniture is well worth preserving, restoring, and reproducing. If you have an early type of house, it will be fun to collect or reproduce some pieces of decorated furniture, and if they are the right kind for your house, they will greatly enhance its character. It is interesting to identify the chief varieties of decorated furniture, to know when and where and by whom it was ornamented, and to appreciate the special quality of this native folk decoration that is a colorful part of our heritage.

The earliest decorated furniture, which was most popular in New England, New York, New Jersey, and Pennsylvania, originated in Connecticut in the latter part of the Pilgrim century. From the luxuriant valley farms near the mouth of the Connecticut River came many interesting painted highboys, chests, and boxes. These pieces, though somewhat reminiscent of Dutch, Flemish, and French decoration, and especially of English crewelwork patterns, have a distinctly American vigor and simplicity of design. The pieces made in and around Guilford are best known today, and the chests of this type, of which quite a number have been found, are popularly referred to as 'Guilford' chests. These were typically made of tulipwood and were built to open from the top with a single decorated front panel over one decorated drawer. The side panels were also painted, most often with a pheasant bordered by a scroll pattern. [9]

In this period the decorator was the 'joiner' who made and carved the furniture. By the mid-eighteenth century, house, coach, and sign painters began to turn to the decoration of furniture, and the furniture maker generally left the finishing of his pieces to these painters, many of whom were itinerants. It is probably because the pioneer furniture was decorated by the men who designed and executed it that painted ornament seems most perfectly correlated with structural design in the early period.

About 1700 the large, boldly ornamented 'Dutch' cupboard was popular in the neighborhood of New York and in the Dutch settlements along the Hudson in New Jersey. One painted cupboard, undoubtedly similar to the priceless example reproduced in Fig. 3, is mentioned in a New York inventory in 1702 as valued at £1.

In New Hampshire about 1720 a number of pieces of painted furniture, somewhat similar to the Guilford chests, were made and ornamented by one Samuel Lane of Hampton Falls. Several simply decorated examples were identified as his by the late Esther Stevens Brazer, the leading authority on early American decoration. A typical blanket chest, found in Hampton and dated 1719, is painted a soft red over which occasional heavy black lines simulate graining. It is decorated with stylized tree forms and a scrolled design with fleur-de-lis patterns executed in black and an enamel-like white.

It may seem surprising that the first settlement at Plymouth did not take the lead in the making of decorated furniture, but the early Puritan dislike of personal and household ornament accounts for this. A quantity of painted furniture was made in Massachusetts, but not before the second quarter of the eighteenth century. Several attractive little chests-on-frame came from around Ipswich, but the outstanding early decorated furniture in Massachusetts was made in the vicinity of Taunton. Here Robert Crosman, a furniture and drum maker and innkeeper by trade, produced a number of delightfully decorated chests, which date from about 1725 to 1740. These so-called 'Taunton chests,' of which we reproduce an example in Fig. 1, were always painted with a vine or tree-of-life design in white, with a few touches of color on a brown or natural wood background. In the later chests

Crosman added birds and tulips and elaborated his delicate tree and vine designs. As in the case of the Guilford chests, these designs are somewhat reminiscent of early English crewel embroidery.

From the mid-eighteenth century in New England we come across interesting examples of painted graining, commonly thought of as a nineteenth-century form of decoration. A fine example is the Connecticut highboy with black graining on a brick-red ground reproduced in Fig. 9.

In the urban centers—Boston, New York, Philadelphia, Salem, and Newport—was found about this time the japanned Chippendale furniture decorated in imitation of Oriental lacquer. In Boston several japanners are recorded as working between 1711 and 1770, and during those years tall-case clocks, highboys, lowboys, and bureaus were elaborately ornamented in this manner. This sort of decoration can scarcely be considered as part of the folk tradition.

In Pennsylvania, in the second half of the eighteenth century, brilliantly painted dower chests were produced in large quantities, as well as other types of decorated furniture. The Pennsylvania Germans, refugees from religious and economic wars, first settled in Germantown and then spread to the southeastern counties of Pennsylvania, bringing with them a rich heritage of old-world peasant design. The chests they made in America and ornamented with typical German and Swiss designs provide our liveliest examples of folk decoration.

Almost every Pennsylvania maiden received a dower chest when she arrived at marriageable age or at her betrothal. This was, of course, an old German custom. The bride's name and the date on which the chest was presented were often lettered on it, and this lettering is always an integral part of the design. The decorative motives were often either symbolic or realistically appropriate for a dower chest, which might be ornamentd with unicorns (which in medieval times were the fabled guardians of maidenhood), a tree-of-life, hearts as symbols of love, or the bride and groom dressed in wedding finery. Even the colors were significant, the popular red and yellow being the colors sacred to Donar, god of marriage and the home.

These chests were painted by professional decorators, some of them itinerants who were kept informed by local gossip in regard to the whereabouts of marriageable daughters. The best known of the Pennsylvania decorators are the Seltzers—Christian and his son John—and his pupils the Ranks—Johann, John Peter, and Peter—all of Columbia County. Christian Seltzer of Jonestown (1747-1831) was an outstanding pioneer decorator, a farmer and innkeeper whose chief interest was the painting of dower chests. His recorded chests are dated from 1771 to 1796, the panel reproduced in Fig. 11 showing his typical signature scratched on a vase with the date 1784. Seltzer's chests are of various designs and combine a variety of motives, all boldly composed and executed with the sweep that distinguishes the hand of a master craftsman. None of his pupils quite came up to Christian Seltzer's work, for though they were exact craftsmen—his son John being especially proficient at mottling and graining—their decoration lacks the variety and the energetic style that mark their master's.

The Pennsylvania chests from the different counties show various distinctive traits, and the origin of a chest can often be discovered if one knows the characteristic details. The Lancaster County chests (see Fig. 17) are of the architectural type with sunken arched panels and columns. The columns are typically painted in two colors, the sunken panels a light cream as a background for tulips, birds, and other motifs. In Lebanon County (see Fig. 14) the tulips are more boldly painted, on panels enclosed by simulated balusters. The panels lack the usual cream ground. Montgomery and Lehigh Counties are best known for the geometric chest designs, in which stylized flower forms are laid out with a compass (see Fig. 13). Berks County is associated with unicorn, horseman, and flower patterns (see Figs. 12 and 22). Columbia County is known for the Seltzer and Rank chests (see Fig. 10), most of which were made in the last decades of the century. These chests are typically decorated with brilliant floral patterns on brown, blue, green, or two-toned grounds, and as more pigments were then available, there is a greater variety of color in these chests than in most of the others.

The Pennsylvania dower chests are a striking product of the homespun folk tradition in early decoration. An opposite tradition, that of sophisticated elegance, is seen in the Adam and Sheraton style furniture, which was popular after the Revolution in both urban and the wealthier rural communities of New England, the Atlantic States, and the South. The fine Adam furniture, made in the last quarter of the eighteenth century and painted with designs in the classic style, does not come into our category of folk decoration; nor does Duncan Phyfe's elaborate gold-leafed furniture of the 1825 period. The Sheraton-type furniture with painted and gold-leafed ornament, which was immensely popular from the 1790's through the first quarter of the nineteenth century, is generally not in the folk tradition.

The Salem sewing table reproduced in Fig. 26, with its stylized landscape and still-life decoration, is an exception that, though somewhat elegant in type, is close to the folk style. The Connecticut drop-leaf table of the same period (Figs. 23 and 24) is a primitive country cousin of our Salem sewing stand, and was probably decorated by some talented lady who learned this painting technique in her seminary days along with watercolor and velvet painting.

About 1820, at the same time that the Sheraton 'fancy chair' was at its height of popularity, the factory era was beginning to change the methods of decoration. At this time stenciling and freehand bronze painting came into use as a substitute for gold-leaf decoration, which was practically abandoned by 1830. In the first period of stenciling the decorators still followed the Sheraton fancy designs, with delicate, fine detail work.

By 1821 Lambert Hitchcock was manufacturing elaborately decorated chairs, which have the stenciled inscription, 'L. Hitchcock, Hitchcocksville, Connecticut, Warranted.' Hitchcocksville, the name he gave the small settlement that grew up around the factory, is now the town of Riverton. About 1826 a brick factory was erected, and approximately a hundred men, women, and children were employed to make and decorate chairs. This factory has recently been re-established to manufacture reproduction Hitchcock chairs. Hitchcock produced enormous numbers of his chairs between 1826 and his death in 1852, and his name has always been associated with the type of chair he originated. Other stencilers whose work is recorded are W. P. Eaton, who had a shop in Boston in 1845, Jarred Johnson, and many more, but their names are for the most part forgotten and the chairs they stenciled are generally known as 'Hitchcock.' These chairs were produced in quantity in the second quarter of the century, mostly in western Connecticut towns, but also throughout New England and in New York and New Jersey. They were sold in stores and peddled from carts for as little as a dollar. The original Hitchcock chairs had rush seats, the backgrounds were usually grained with black or brown over an undercoat of red, striping was in yellow or white paint, and the bronze-powder stencil designs were very elaborate. By 1830 stenciling methods were greatly simplified. The number of stencils was reduced so that the design could be applied in two or three parts instead of the dozens that made up the earlier composite stencil patterns. About 1840 colored bronze powders came on the market, stencils were cut in one piece to lower costs, and the delicate shading of the earlier work was seldom used. The growing demand for quick and easy work methods determined the evolution of stencil decoration in America.

Stenciled furniture was in general a conventional factory product in the second quarter of the nineteenth century. This was not so in the case of the furniture painted by a group of independent folk decorators who were working in rural New England and Pennsylvania during the same period.

The original, native New England folk decoration is typically represented by the gray-green chest with crudely stylized trees reproduced in Fig. 7, which, like the earlier wall cupboard shown in Fig. 32, was very likely painted by one of the house decorators whose work is illustrated in Chapter 5. A number of strikingly ornamented sailor's chests were painted by their owners in the New England seacoast towns; one of these is a unique sea-green blanket chest, made in Nantucket, which was covered with primitive whaling scenes.

In Pennsylvania we find quantities of provincial painted furniture, some good examples of which are reproduced in Figs. 4, 25, and 31.

In these, as in the earlier dower chests, we find old-world devices such as tulips, hearts, angels, and parrots; and even in the two-toned decoration seen in Figs. 21 and 22, tulip and geometrical designs emerge from the swirls of paint. An all-American design such as the Andrew Jackson desk shown in Fig. 25 is exceptional. The Mahantango Valley pieces by Jacob Maser, Braun, and other decorators are outstanding from the point of view of folk design (see Fig. 31); and the simple painted chairs like the one seen in Fig. 27 are most attractive and usable for any home.

Furniture decorated with freehand painting, stenciling, and two-toned finishes continued to be popular in the third quarter of the nineteenth century in all parts of the country. The stencils found in the loft of Dyke Mill at Montague, Massachusetts, at one time a furniture factory, are typical of the best late stencil designs (see p. 19). The later decorated furniture, however, does not often have the originality and vitality of design that distinguish the earlier pieces. A chest like the one made for a girl named Anne Beer in 1790 (Fig. 19) is a fine example of imaginative folk design. The wavy branches of flowers borne by the mermaids suggest fabulous seaweed blossoms, and even the lettering carries out the fluid, rhythmic quality of the whole pattern and each of its parts. It is a masterpiece of folk decoration, and one finds a few comparable examples after the middle of the nineteenth century. The craftsman's individual talent was then too often standardized by a mass-production approach, and the Victorian era with its invention of the wood-carving machine virtually ended painted and stenciled furniture decoration in America.

Methods of Decoration

FREEHAND OR BRUSH-STROKE PAINTING

The process of painting designs on furniture without the use of stencils needs no general description. Many kinds of designs and even simple landscapes were painted freehand on furniture from the seventeenth through the nineteenth centuries, as may be seen from the plates that illustrate this chapter.

Some of the freehand painting was of the brush-stroke variety commonly used for decorating tin.

Brush-stroke painting requires practice and patience. The old-time decorator served many years as an apprentice before he mastered the skillfully formed brush strokes and the even composition found on many of the old pieces.

Most leaf strokes are made with a single stroke of the brush. A flower is represented by several brush strokes. When a very wide section appears, it is made by several full-width strokes. For types of brushes see p. 3.

For brush-stroke painting use a ¾ inch square-tipped, No. 1 quill brush fitted to a short wooden handle for the smaller design details. For larger units use a No. 4 lettering brush or a bigger quill brush.

Use a folded piece of wax paper as a palette. Squeeze out a small dab of japan tube paint. Artists' oil colors can be added to japan colors to get the desired tints. Add a few drops of turpentine to soften. Mix thoroughly to make sure the pigment is dissolved. Keep about a tablespoon of varnish in a small jar top and add to the pigment as needed for smooth flowing. Dip the brush in the mixed paint and stroke the brush full length on the palette to wipe off excess. Watch for grains of paint or dust specks. Should any appear, clean the brush in Carbona and try again. Experience will teach you when just enough paint remains in the brush for a clean brush stroke.

Heavy pressure on a brush will broaden the stroke, release will lighten the line. An even line requires even pressure the length of the line.

To Decorate Taunton Chest Shown

Note: The old-time decorators used a slow-drying oil medium for both background and design painting. Linseed oil, turpentine, and pigment were mixed to the desired colors and allowed to dry as long as two weeks between operations. Varnish was never used on most of these old chests. They were finished by repeated rubbing

with oil. This is the process described for the Taunton chest.

In the case of Pennsylvania chests, because of the variety of colors used, considerably more time is required if one wishes to decorate in the old technique. The process described on p. 15, using flat oil or japan paint for the background and design, is quicker and the result approximates the early decoration. However, if an authentic finish is desired regardless of time involved, proceed as for the Taunton chest.

In decorating these chests the main thing to keep in mind is that the slow, old-time method uses pigment mixed with oil and turpentine for the background as well as the decoration. For the quicker method, the background is painted with a flat paint, or japan, and the decoration is done with the same kind of paints, toned with artists' oils if necessary.

1. Prepare surface for painting according to instructions in the Introduction, p. 4.

2. With a piece of chalk mark in the main lines of the design and check to see that the decoration is well balanced on the chest. Go over the chalk lines with a sharp-pointed instrument. These will show through the background paint and be a guide for painting the design. Wipe off chalk.

3. Give chest first coat of MEDIUM BROWN. Allow to dry 2 weeks.

4. Give chest second coat of MEDIUM BROWN and allow to dry 2 weeks.

DETAIL OF TAUNTON CHEST—See Fig. 1

5. Following pattern, paint all of the design WHITE, using a small quill brush and a No. 2 scroll brush for the long stems and fine lines. Let dry 4 days.

6. With a small quill brush, apply dabs of VERMILION to tulip centers, birds' beaks, and tips of scrolls, and touch inside medallions. Allow to dry thoroughly.

7. Antique according to instructions for wood without a varnish coat, p. 7.

COLOR GUIDE

MEDIUM BROWN—burnt umber and Venetian red, lightened with a small amount of yellow ochre and mixed with ⅔ raw linseed oil and ⅓ turpentine, with a touch of japan dryer.

All scroll work and white sections, WHITE. toned with raw umber, mixed as above.

Red markings VERMILION, mixed with oil and turpentine as for the brown, and thick enough so as not to drip.

In addition to materials listed in Introduction under 'How to Prepare Wood for Decoration,' p. 4, you will need the following:

Materials	Where to buy	Amount
Paints (in oil):		
Burnt umber	Paint store	½ pt.
Venetian red	Paint store	½ pt.
Yellow ochre	Art supply store	1 tube
Raw umber	Art supply store	1 tube
Titan white	Art supply store	1 tube
Vermilion	Art supply store	1 tube
Brushes:		
No. 0 quill	Art supply store	1
No. 2 scroll	Art supply store	1
1½″ background	Hardware store	1
Raw linseed oil	Hardware store	1 qt.
Turpentine	Hardware store	1 pt.
Japan dryer	Art supply store	1 oz.
Chalk	Stationery store	1
Embroidery punch	Notions	1

To Decorate Pennsylvania Dower Chest Shown

1. Prepare surface for painting according to instructions in the Introduction, p. 4.

2. With a piece of chalk outline panels on bare wood, spacing them accurately. Examine from a distance to see that units are well balanced. If the panels look right, go over the chalk lines with a sharp instrument. These lines will serve as a guide after the chest is painted. Wipe off chalk.

3. Give background first coat of DULL RED, working carefully around the panels you have outlined. Let dry 24 hours.

4. Give background second coat of DULL RED. Let dry 24 hours.

5. Apply first coat of flat WHITE to panels. Let dry 24 hours.

6. Apply second coat of flat WHITE to panels. Let dry 24 hours.

7. Enlarge and apply the design according to instructions in Introduction, p. 5. It will be easier to draw in the design, as well as to decorate, if the chest is laid on its back.

8. Paint the design, following color description below.

Using a No. 6 showcard brush or large quill, paint vases DARK GRAY. Paint flower stamens, leaves, and stems RED BROWN, using a scroll brush for the stems and large quill for the leaves. With smaller quill brush paint tip of lower flower buds with YELLOW OCHRE. Let dry.

Paint inner petals of lower buds, sections of upper flowers shown with dots, lower petals, and center of single flower BLUE GRAY.

Paint narrow stripe around the design BLUE GRAY, using a striper.

Paint in the outlines of border scroll in RED, using a No. 4 scroll brush.

Let dry 24 hours.

With quill brush, paint remaining petals in lower buds, missing sections of top flowers, and dots on gray petals, VERMILION.

Fill in the border scroll with BLUE GRAY.

Paint feet and lower edge of molding BLACK.

The molding around lid and the base molding as yet unpainted are BLUE GRAY.

Allow to dry thoroughly, then varnish. Let dry 24 hours and antique according to instructions for light background, p. 7. Apply two more coats of varnish 24 hours apart and when the last coat has dried 48 hours, rub with powdered pumice and crude oil.

Note: Keep in a tight jar a reserve of background paint, which may be used for retouching if necessary.

COLOR GUIDE

DULL RED—vermilion in japan mixed with alizarin crimson and raw umber.

Materials	Where to buy	Amount
Paints:		
Vermilion in japan	Art supply store	½ pt.
Burnt umber in japan	Art supply store	1 tube
Raw umber in oil	Art supply store	1 tube
Yellow ochre in oil	Art supply store	1 tube
Alizarin crimson in oil	Art supply store	1 tube
Venetian red in oil	Art supply store	1 tube
Prussian blue in oil	Art supply store	1 tube
Titan white in oil	Art supply store	1 tube
Flat black	Hardware store	½ pt.
Flat white	Hardware store	½ pt.
Brushes:		
No. 6 showcard or No. 3 large quill	Art supply store	1
No. 1 small quill	Art supply store	1
No. 4 scroll	Art supply store	1
2″ varnish	Art supply store	1
2″ background	Art supply store	1
Striper	Art supply store	1
Chalk	Stationery store	1
Embroidery punch	Notions	1
Turpentine	Hardware store	1 pt.
Powdered pumice	Art supply store	1 oz.
Crude oil	Art supply store	1 pt.
Varnish	Art supply store	1 pt.

DARK GRAY—flat black or japan black mixed with white.

RED BROWN—burnt umber in japan, or artists' oil color, mixed with Venetian red.

BLUE GRAY—Prussian blue mixed with raw umber and white.

RED—alizarin crimson with a bit of raw umber.

VERMILION—toned to dull shade with raw umber.

YELLOW OCHRE

In addition to materials listed in Introduction under 'How to Prepare Wood for Decoration,' p. 4, and 'How to Enlarge and Apply Pattern to Surface,' p. 5, you will need the following:

PANEL OF PENNSYLVANIA DOWER CHEST—See Figs. 10 and 11

To Decorate Painted Chair Shown

1. Prepare chair for decoration according to instructions in the Introduction, p. 4.

2. Paint chair STRAW YELLOW, using light-yellow flat oil paint and tinting to straw color with yellow ochre and raw umber. Allow to dry 24 hours.

3. Give chair second coat of yellow paint and allow to dry 24 hours.

4. Enlarge and apply the design according to instructions in Introduction, p. 5.

5. Paint the slat design, following color description below. Read 'Freehand or Brush-Stroke Painting,' p. 12. Use a large quill brush for large areas, and for scrolls and veinings a No. 2 scroll brush. Use a small quill for dots. Paint base designs first and allow to dry before adding lines and dots. Plan to do all sections of each color at one time, because it may be difficult to match colors later.

Berries and flowers, VERMILION.

Large leaves, all small leaves, tendrils, and stems, DARK GREEN.

Seeds and flower stamens, CHROME YELLOW.

Veinings, LAMP BLACK.

6. Wait till the slat is dry so as not to smudge, then paint chair uprights, arrow spindles, leg stretcher, and seat roll with heart design in DARK GREEN; tip with VERMILION dot. In circular design petals alternate DARK GREEN and VERMILION. Let dry 24 hours.

7. The legs and upright turnings have wide bands of color. Using a No. 6 showcard brush, apply DARK GREEN to bottom turning, VERMILION to center turning, and RED-BROWN stripes to top turning, as indicated. Let dry 24 hours.

8. Apply one varnish coat. Let dry 24 hours.

9. Using RED-BROWN and a striping brush, apply wide band down each front leg. Apply narrow RED-BROWN stripes to slat, around chair seat, bordering uprights, leg stretcher, and arrow spindles. Let dry 24 hours.

10. Apply second varnish coat, let dry 24 hours, then antique, following instructions on p. 7 for light backgrounds.

11. Give two more coats of varnish, 24 hours apart. Let last coat dry 48 hours.

12. Finish by rubbing with soft cloth, dipped in pumice and crude oil.

Note: Mix sufficient quantity of paint to complete chair. Keep stored in tight container.

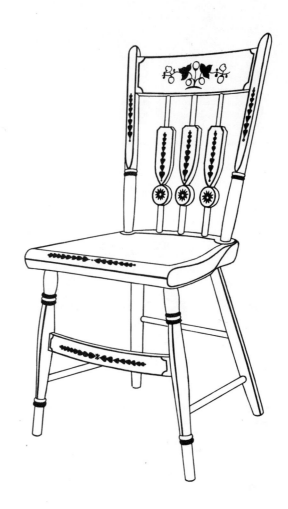

COLOR GUIDE

VERMILION

CHROME YELLOW—chrome yellow medium toned with raw umber to mustard shade.

DARK GREEN—either chrome green medium toned with raw umber, or chrome yellow medium mixed with plenty of Prussian blue and raw umber to deep-green shade.

RED BROWN—burnt umber with Venetian red.

In addition to the materials listed in Introduction under preparing wood for decoration, p. 4, and enlarging and transferring design, p. 5, you will need the following:

Materials	Where to buy	Amount	Materials	Where to buy	Amount
Paints:			Brushes:		
Light-yellow flat	Paint store	½ pt.	Large quill, or		
Vermilion in japan	Art supply store	1 tube	No. 6 showcard	Art supply store	1
Chrome yellow medium			No. 2 scroll	Art supply store	1
in japan	Art supply store	1 tube	No. 1 striping quill	Art supply store	1
Lamp black in oil	Art supply store	1 tube	No. 1 small quill	Art supply store	1
Yellow ochre in oil	Art supply store	1 tube	1½″ background	Art supply store	1
Raw umber in oil	Art supply store	1 tube	1½″ varnish	Art supply store	1
Chrome green medium			Varnish	Art supply store	½ pt.
in japan, or	Art supply store	1 tube	Pumice	Art supply store	1 oz.
Prussian blue in oil	Art supply store	1 tube	Crude oil	Art supply store	1 qt.
Burnt umber in oil	Art supply store	1 tube	Turpentine	Hardware store	1 pt.
Venetian red in oil	Art supply store	1 tube			

DETAILS OF PAINTED CHAIR—See Fig. 27

STENCILING

Cutting the Stencil

Trace the design on a piece of frosted acetate tracing material (Supersee or a similar material). Examine to see whether any two units of the design touch and whether one seems to pass behind the other. Each unit must have a separate stencil, unless it is a repeat such as a grape or a leaf.

Where each unit is free-standing (not touching or built up from behind) the stencil may be cut in one piece.

After determining how many separate units there are in your design, you are ready to trace the units on architects' linen and to cut your stencil.

Place a small piece of architects' linen over the design, dull side up, and trace carefully with India ink and a crow-quill pen. Be sure to allow

STENCILS FOUND IN THE LOFT OF DYKE MILL AT MONTAGUE, MASS. Courtesy *Antiques*

at least a 1-inch border all around each separate unit. This is necessary to protect surrounding areas when bronze powder is being applied.

To cut the stencil use very sharp-pointed surgical or embroidery scissors with a straight blade and an Exacto No. 11 or No. 16 knife with replaceable blade. Keep scissors and blades sharp.

When cutting a segment, such as a leaf or fruit, puncture the center and then use the scissors to cut out the segment. Should only a portion of fruit or other unit be visible, complete the whole fruit or leaf.

For fine lines and stems, cut one side with the knife and then use the scissors to pare it to the desired width. The secret of a good stencil is to have clean-cut, flat edges.

Place a piece of window glass under the linen when cutting with the knife. Sharpen the cutting edge frequently on a carborundum stone.

Small dots or circles may be punched with a large needle and the edge trimmed with scissors on the reverse side, and smoothed with No. 00 sandpaper.

Mend any break in the stencil with scotch tape on both sides of the stencil.

Materials	Where to buy	Amount
Architects' tracing linen	Art supply store	½ yd.
Frosted acetate tracing material (Supersee or similar material)	Art supply store	½ yd.
Embroidery or surgical scissors	Cutlery store	1 pr.
No. 11 or No. 16 Exacto knife	Art supply store	1
Window glass	Hardware store	1 pane
Carborundum stone	Hardware store	1
India ink	Stationery store	1 bottle
Crow-quill pen	Art supply store	1
Scotch tape	Stationery store	1 roll
No. 00 sandpaper	Hardware store	1 sheet
Large needle	Notions	1

Applying the design

Be sure background paint has had at least 24 hours to dry before applying the stencil.

Give part to be decorated a thin, evenly spread coat of varnish.

For proper drying, varnish requires clear weather and a room temperature of at least 70°.

Let dry until set (from 30 minutes to 3 hours, depending upon the drying condition of the weather). When ready to use, the varnish will be only slightly sticky when tested with the finger, and the finger will come away clean.

Meantime assemble materials. Place small mounds of the bronze powders on a piece of upholsterers' velour or velvet. This will keep the powder from flying about, and when you are finished, the powder may be folded in the velour and put away for future use.

Place surface to be decorated in a horizontal position, and when the varnish has reached the proper stage, lay the stencil in place and press it down lightly until it adheres to the varnish. When using a stencil composed of more than one unit, start with the center unit or central section, and work out toward each end.

Wrap a piece of silk velvet or soft chamois over the end of the index finger. Dip cautiously into the powder, applying a few grains at a time to the stencil. Use a gentle circular motion and work from the edge to the center, building up to the desired amount of brightness and shading. Use caution in applying the powder. It is easier to build up with a few grains at a time than to remove a splotch that is too bright. For tiny leaves and fine lines the stencil will need to be well filled with the powder; always apply only a few grains at a time.

After dipping into the powder, tap the finger on a clean spot of the velour to shake off the excess powder.

Be sure no powder remains on the stencil or it will fly off onto the background when the stencil is lifted.

After use, clean the stencil thoroughly on both sides with cleaning fluid.

Slight mistakes in powder spills may be wiped out, while varnish is wet, with a lintless cloth dipped in varnish.

Another method is to let the varnish dry completely and paint out the error with the same paint you used for the background, using a small brush. This touching-up will not show after the final coat of varnish is applied.

Do not varnish until bronze powder has had at least 48 hours to dry. Before varnishing, go over piece with a damp cloth to remove excess powder.

Materials	Where to buy	Amount
Upholsterers' velour	Upholstery shop	¼ yd.
Silk velvet or soft chamois	Art supply store	Small piece
Cleaning fluid	Art supply store	1 bottle
Varnish	Art supply store	½ pt.
1½" brush	Art supply store	1
Bronze powders	Art supply store	1 oz. each

To Decorate Hitchcock-Type Chair Shown

1. Copy pattern and enlarge as described in Introduction, p. 5.

2. Cut stencils in units as shown, according to directions on p. 18.

3. Prepare surface for painting (see p. 4).

4. Apply undercoat of dull red (Venetian red in japan) mixed to a creamy consistency in turpentine. Paint entire chair except the main slat, which will carry the stencil. On this use flat black. Allow to dry 24 hours.

5. Apply flat black thinned with turpentine over the portions of the chair you have painted red. To obtain a grained effect pull a piece of crumpled mosquito netting, newspaper, or stiff cloth across each section of the chair as it is painted. If the desired effect is not obtained, wipe off immediately and try the graining again.

The slat to carry the design should now receive a second coat of flat black paint. Allow to dry 24 hours.

6. Give the slat to be stenciled a thin coat of varnish. Allow to dry to the sticky stage (see p. 20. 'Applying the Design'). While you are waiting for the varnish to dry sufficiently to apply the stencil, read carefully directions on applying bronze powder, p. 20. Get ready the materials you will need. Have the bronze powders mentioned below in a small mound on a piece of upholsterers' velour, and the piece of silk velvet or soft chamois fitted to your finger.

7. To apply the stencil, begin with the fruit-bowl unit and place it in the center of the slat. Using pale-gold bronze powder, rub your finger gently over the stencil, working from the center and shading to the ends. The sides of the bowl are formed by placing the curved edge of the bowl unit (left edge of stencil) in position and gently rubbing powder against the curve.

Place pear stencil in proper position and highlight the center by applying powder with a circular motion. To define the edge of the fruit, touch the edge of the stencil lightly, working

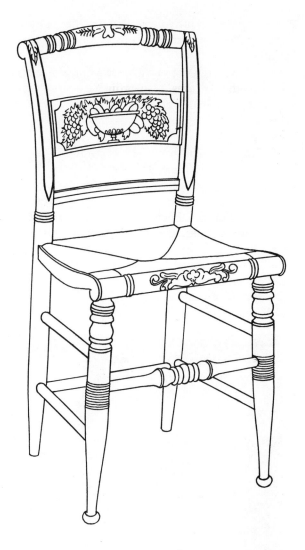

from the outside edge toward the center.

Follow with each peach section, rubbing more firmly where highlight is indicated.

Place fruit at base of bowl and grape stems in position, applying powder as described above.

Now, using a mixture of aluminum and statuary bronze and the large-grape pattern, apply powder to each grape, moving the unit along to

[21]

build up the bunch according to the pattern. The smaller-grape stencil is used for the bottom grapes.

Starting at the center of the bowl again, place the leaves according to pattern (see drawing), applying the pale-gold bronze powder to the tips and shading toward the center. Allow to dry overnight.

8. Apply design to upright parts, top of chair, and front of seat frame. These may be traced and gold leaf applied according to directions on p. 25. The vertical design on uprights may well be omitted. For the beginner fearful of handling gold leaf, the design may be painted on as described for gold leaf and, when almost dry, pale-gold powder rubbed over the surface with velvet. Let dry 24 hours.

9. Apply a coat of varnish and allow to dry 24 hours.

10. Add leaf veins to stenciled design, and markings on gold leaf, using a small quill brush and lamp black mixed with a bit of varnish. The tendrils are painted in freehand, with a scroll brush; use chrome yellow medium in japan toned with raw umber; thin with turpentine, and add a touch of varnish.

11. Paint turnings with a mixture of pale-gold bronze lining powder and varnish, using a No. 6 showcard brush. Carry gold only three-quarters of the way around turnings.

12. Stripe with toned yellow in japan according to directions on p. 6. Let dry 24 hours.

13. Apply three coats of varnish, allowing 24 hours to dry between each coat. The first two coats over design section may contain a small bit of raw umber to antique. The last coat of varnish is applied clear.

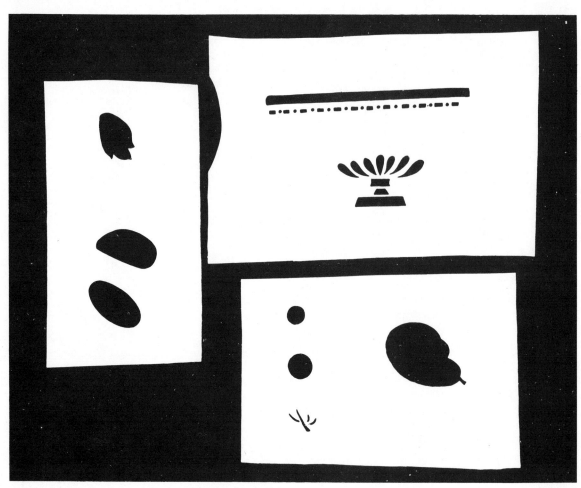

STENCILS FOR HITCHCOCK-TYPE CHAIR—See Fig. 30

14. Allow to dry 48 hours and then rub with a mixture of powdered pumice and crude oil for a soft, mellow glow.

In addition to materials listed under 'How to Prepare Wood for Decoration,' p. 4, 'To Enlarge Design,' p. 5, 'Cutting the Stencil,' p. 18, and 'Applying the Design,' p. 20, you will need the following:

Materials	Where to buy	Amount
Paints:		
Venetian red in japan	Art supply store	½ pt.
Lamp black	Art supply store	1 tube
Flat black	Paint store	½ pt.
Chrome yellow medium in japan	Art supply store	1 tube
Yellow ochre in japan	Art supply store	1 tube
Raw umber in oil	Art supply store	1 tube
Brushes:		
1½"-2" background	Art supply store	1
No. 6 showcard	Art supply store	1
No. 1 striping quill	Art supply store	1
No. 0 quill	Art supply store	1
No. 2 scroll	Art supply store	1
1½"-2" varnish	Art supply store	1
Bronze powders:		
Pale gold	Art supply store	1 oz.
Pale-gold lining	Art supply store	1 oz.
Aluminum	Art supply store	1 oz.
Statuary	Art supply store	1 oz.
Gold leaf	Art supply store	1 book
Black Serviseal	Art supply store	½ pt.
Varnish	Art supply store	½ pt.
Pumice	Art supply store	1 oz.
Crude oil	Art supply store	1 pt.
Turpentine	Paint store	1 pt.
Stiff cloth or newspaper		

TWO-TONED FINISHES

Graining

Red under black or brown, used as early as the eighteenth century and commonly used on Hitchcock chairs and Boston rockers, also on woodwork and accessories.

Apply undercoat of dull red (Venetian red in japan) mixed to a creamy consistency in turpentine. Allow to dry 24 hours.

Apply flat black thinned with turpentine. While it is wet, wipe off quickly with a piece of crumpled mosquito netting or some other stiff cloth. Crumpled newspaper, cellophane, or a wad of No. 3 steel wool may be used. A leather comb was sometimes used by the early decorators.

Tortoise Shell

Red under black or brown. Used on some Sheraton chairs and other pieces. Undercoat of dull red (Venetian red in japan) mixed to a creamy consistency in turpentine. Allow to dry 24 hours.

Apply a thin coat of flat black thinned with turpentine; while it is wet, take an almost dry brush and strike the wet paint in an irregular fashion, leaving some places quite red and others black.

A description from a treatise on ornamental painting published in 1841 reads: 'To Paint Turtle Shell. Make the ground work dark with Venetian red, and rose pink and lampblack, which will form a dark reddish brown; then take a coarse sponge wet in water, dipped in Venetian ground fine in varnish, dot it on the work, then take rose pink and apply it as before. Give two coats varnish.'

Vinegar Painting (Putty Graining)

Commonly found on yellow-painted, wood-seat chairs in the mid-nineteenth century. Also on chests.

Paint background soft yellow. (Mix flat white, yellow ochre, and touch of raw umber until a soft straw color is attained. Then add a little chrome yellow.) Allow to dry 24 hours.

Apply a coat of variegated brown (made by mixing burnt-umber in vinegar) to the chair seat or the chest. Work in patches of burnt umber and raw umber. While the paint is still wet, take a roll of putty and roll it around in a circle formation to make fans and other designs. A border of wheel-like units may be made by stamping with the end of putty roll.

Marbling

A smoked effect, found for the most part on Pennsylvania chairs, and also on boxes, bellows, et cetera.

Give two or three coats of flat white. Allow to dry 24 hours between each coat.

Apply a coat of varnish and when it is almost dry, pass a lighted candle near the surface quickly enough for the smoke to adhere. Care must be taken to pass the candle quickly enough to blacken but not to blister the varnish.

Mottling–Sponging–Stippling

Found on many eighteenth- and nineteenth-century Pennsylvania and New England chests and accessories.

Use a coarse sponge, dip in thick paint, and touch evenly on the dry background. (On Pennsylvania chests this was usually done in the background color around the white panels.)

A circular pattern may be made on a freshly painted dark surface on a light ground by using the end of a dry corn cob and twisting it around to make a circular pattern in the paint.

A seaweed effect was made by mixing raw linseed oil with one of the partly transparent colors. This was applied after the background paint had been allowed to dry 24 hours. Then, with a 2-inch brush dipped in turpentine, figures were worked in the wet paint. The turpentine superimposed upon the oil color made it separate into curious fern-like figures.

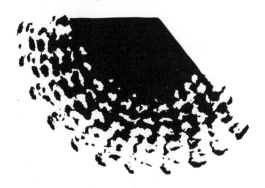

Scumbling

Commonly used on nineteenth-century chests.

A light color in transparent or semi-transparent glaze over an opaque underpainting. For instance, an underpainting of yellow (ochre and white mixed together) and a glaze of raw linseed oil, thinned with an equal amount of turpentine and japan drier and lightly tinted with umber. Allow the undercoat to dry 24 hours. Then with a brush or a folded-cloth swab, apply the glaze freely. Using a brush, with a light touch draw off excess glazing fluid to make the desired pattern.

Feather Painting

Found on nineteenth-century chests and also on woodwork.

Follow instructions for scumbling given above, but instead of using a brush to draw off the excess fluid, use a feather. Various-sized feathers may be used to work in the design. Take a long, supple tail feather and draw it across the glaze, ending with a hook or curl. Also try a short, stubby feather to achieve the desired effect.

Finger Painting

Found on eighteenth- and nineteenth-century Pennsylvania and New England chests and boxes.

The background paint is allowed to dry 24 hours. Then apply a coat of a darker color, and with the thumb and heel of your hand make swirls in the wet paint. Designs may also be made with a finger.

JAPANNING

Japanning in America was an imitation of the Oriental lacquer work found on furniture from China and India. English craftsmen were imitating Oriental lacquer work as early as the sixteenth century. Chippendale, Hepplewhite, and Sheraton all designed furniture to be japanned.

In America the Chippendale pieces designed for japanning were highboys, lowboys, mirrors, and clocks. Some of the japanned furniture used by the American colonists was imported from England, but there were craftsmen skilled in japanning here before the eighteenth century.

The art of japanning is an extremely complicated process. Esther Stevens Brazer, in her book *Early American Decoration*, devotes a chapter to this technique. It is suggested that the reader refer to Mrs. Brazer's book for information on japanning.

GOLD-LEAF DECORATION

Gold leaf was used extensively on fine trays, Sheraton fancy chairs, and some Hitchcocks.

Gold leaf comes in various shades in book form, with or without backing. In combination patterns it is applied before other sections of the design.

To apply gold leaf, the design is first painted in freehand with black Serviseal varnish. When it is almost dry, the leaf is picked up with wax-paper backing and laid face down on varnish sizing. It is then rubbed gently with a pad of cotton and when backing is lifted, the design is polished further with cotton, and excess gold removed.

Etched designs are then applied with a sharp instrument.

Shading with thin overtones of burnt sienna or umber is applied after first coat of varnish, and details such as leaf veins are painted in with lamp black and a fine brush.

FREEHAND BRONZE PAINTING

Freehand bronze painting was used by the master decorators on fine furniture and trays in the mid-eighteenth and early nineteenth centuries.

Paint in the design with black Serviseal or japan colors thinned with turpentine and a bit of varnish. Apply thinly and allow to become almost dry.

With a pointed tip of velvet or charcoal stump, dip in the gold powder and apply the highlights to the design. If background is black, tips and edges are highlighted in bronze. If background is light, the design is highlighted in the center, which leaves dark edges to define the design.

After three days, wash with water to remove any surplus powder.

1. TAUNTON CHEST

2. GUILFORD CHEST

3. 'DUTCH' CUPBOARD

4. PENNSYLVANIA DRESSER

5. PENNSYLVANIA CHEST OF DRAWERS

6. NEW ENGLAND CHEST OF DRAWERS

[27]

7. NEW ENGLAND
BLANKET CHEST

8. NEW ENGLAND CHEST

9. CONNECTICUT HIGHBOY

10, 11. PENNSYLVANIA DOWER CHEST
AND DETAIL OF PANEL

12.

13.

12, 13, 14. PENNSYLVANIA DOWER CHESTS

15

16

17

15, 16, 17. PENNSYLVANIA DOWER CHESTS

18

19

20

[33]

18, 19, 20. PENNSYLVANIA DOWER CHESTS

21. PENNSYLVANIA BED

22. PENNSYLVANIA
BLANKET CHEST

[34]

23, 24. CONNECTICUT TABLE AND DETAIL OF TOP

[35]

25. PENNSYLVANIA SLANT-TOP DESK

26. SALEM SEWING TABLE

27. PENNSYLVANIA ARROW-BACK CHAIR

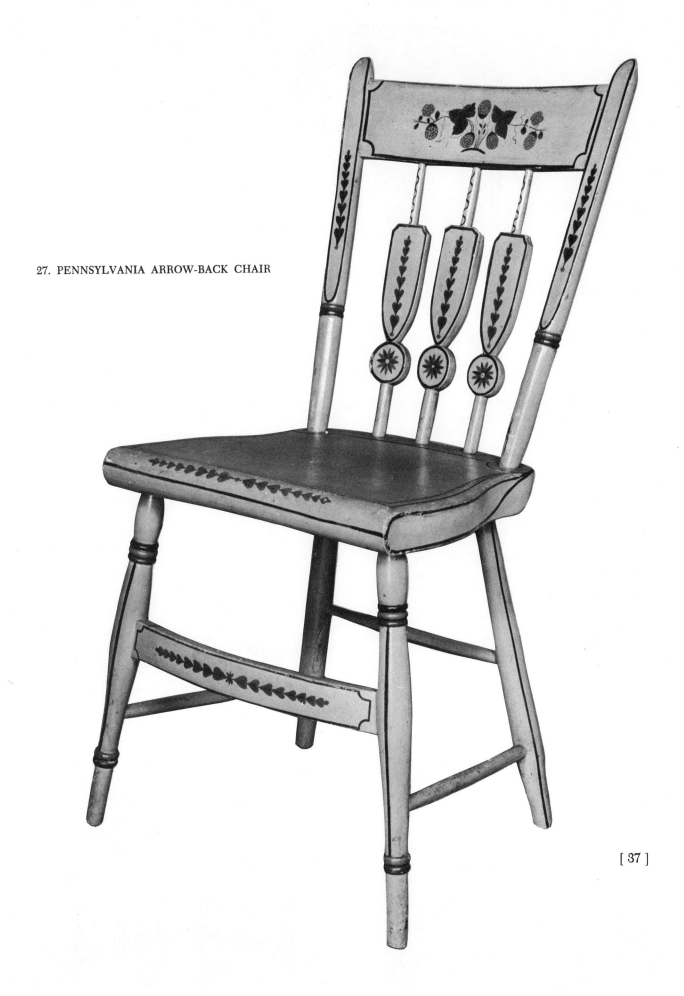

28. PENNSYLVANIA BALLOON-BACK CHAIR

29. DETAIL OF NEW ENGLAND CHAIR

30. HITCHCOCK-TYPE CHAIR

31. PENNSYLVANIA
TALL CLOCK

32. CONNECTICUT WALL CUPBOARD

33. PENNSYLVANIA STOOL

CHAPTER 2

DECORATIVE ACCESSORIES

Early Examples and Modern Adaptations

Many decorative accessories were used in early households, and quantities of them were ornamented with painted or stenciled designs. A selection of typical objects illustrates this chapter.

The boxes—for candles, knives, documents, salt, trinkets, and other personal belongings—are the most interesting group. They were made in large quantities in New England and Pennsylvania and show the usual regional differences. Decorated boxes, old ones or reproductions, make useful gifts for anyone interested in antiques. The Pennsylvania candle and document boxes with sliding lids are a good size for storing packages of cigarettes and matches, and the small, trunk-shaped boxes with latched tops are just right to hold a dozen cigarettes. A trinket box is as useful as ever for jewelry and is attractive as a bureau accessory. One of the larger boxes, such as the one described on p. 42 and reproduced in Fig. 34, would make a fine decorative container for cards in the game room, for paper napkins in the dining room, or for writing equipment in the study. The Pennsylvania bride's boxes, which are one to two feet long, are also useful for storing things and are most decorative.

The painted bride's boxes were made in Pennsylvania at about the same time as the dower chests, mostly in the late 1700's. The box is made of light wood stretched round an oval base, to which it is attached by small nails or pegs. The piece forming the frame is secured by a wooden or rawhide thong. The lid fits down over the framework to a depth of about an inch. The decoration and lettering on these boxes bear out the tradition that they were gifts from the bridegroom to his bride, intended for the more fragile items of her trousseau. In the homeland elaborately ornamented objects were habitually given by the lover to his prospective bride, and this custom was carried over by the German and German-speaking Swiss emigrants to Pennsylvania. Some of the boxes are decorated with fruits, flowers, or conventionalized designs, some with a horseman or a single standing figure, more with figures of the bride and groom. In general the Swiss type of decoration is more delicate and graceful than the German, which is heavier in form and coloring. A considerable number of bride's boxes were brought over from Europe, either by the emigrants or, later, by dealers. The imported boxes are as a rule more elaborately decorated than those made in Pennsylvania.

A number of German inscriptions found on bride's boxes were translated by Esther Stevens Brazer for an article in the magazine *Antiques*. One of these reads: 'Those who love in honor, no man can put asunder.' Another: 'All young ladies on this earth would like well to become wives.' One box shows a bride and groom seated on a bench near a fire over which hangs a cauldron, and the homely inscription reads: 'I will go now, my dear Fritz, and cook you some nice apple sauce.' A box, evidently made for a confirmed spinster instead of for the bride, is lettered, 'To be alone for myself shall be my pleasure.' The box reproduced in Fig. 45 is inscribed, 'The hand of love makes a firm tight bond.'

Figs. 38, 39, and 40 show a unique Pennsylvania pine trinket box decorated with inset panels containing fractur-type watercolors on paper mounted under glass. The wood was originally painted Indian red; the colors on the papered panels are blue, scarlet, yellow, green, brown, and pink. The front views are supposed to represent three brothers who married three sisters.

A good many small decorated chests have been found. The late eighteenth-century one from Deerfield, Massachusetts, (Fig. 37) is one of the most interesting. An early American finger-painting artist decorated this chest in two tones of brown with a lively scene of an Indian raid on a colonial home.

In the late eighteenth century in New England, two-toned decoration was also applied to picture frames, and well-preserved examples of marbleized frames have been found. An early two-toned picture frame from Pennsylvania is shown in Fig. 67. A later Pennsylvania frame, Fig. 66, is painted with a freehand design in yellow and red on black. The stenciled New England frame shown in Fig. 68 is described on p. 47. These decorated frames can easily be reproduced and will greatly enhance an old painting or print.

The miniature dough trough from Pennsylvania described on p. 44 and reproduced in Figs. 47 and 48 is decorated with an especially charming folk design. This piece, accurately copied, would make a delightful stool for a child's room, or for any country bedroom or living room.

There are various kinds of decorated wooden ware that can be reproduced for numbers of purposes. The bucket we describe on p. 45 and illustrate in Fig. 50 would be simple and inexpensive to duplicate. Unpainted wooden buckets can be bought for about a dollar in most hardware stores; decorated with Pennsylvania designs, they make perfect waste baskets or picnic hampers. The wooden saffron and salt containers made in quantities in the last half of the nineteenth century by Joseph Lehn, a retired farmer from Lancaster County, make fine cigarette containers for informal luncheon or porch tables. This type of wooden ware is turned on a lathe. Modern reproductions should be painted in the original gay colors, most often red, leaf-green, yellow, black, and white on a dull pink or yellow ground. Details of any of these designs are most effective painted on wooden utensils such as salad sets and wooden bowls.

The pieces we have mentioned so far, except for the stenciled frame, were painted freehand. Stenciled decoration is seen on the bellows (Fig. 65), on the cornices for Venetian blinds (Figs. 56 and 57), and on the clock and mirror reproduced in Figs. 59 and 62. A number of the clocks and mirrors featured painted glass decoration, which is not so difficult to reproduce as one might expect. As the glasses of many of the old clocks and mirrors that one buys are missing or damaged, it is useful to know how to do reverse painting on glass. These glass paintings may also be framed to hang as pictures. The New England glass painting we describe on p. 48 and reproduce in Fig. 60 was most likely a clock glass, but it had been framed many years ago and is an engaging primitive painting in its own right.

Kinds of Decoration

FREEHAND PAINTING

Found on boxes, buckets, dough troughs, spoon racks, bellows, picture frames, wooden ware, hearth and clothes brushes, et cetera. The same kind of freehand painting used for furniture was done on accessories, and also brush-stroke painting as used on furniture and tin, described on p. 12.

To Decorate Pennsylvania Box Shown

1. To prepare the box for decoration read instructions on 'How to Prepare Wood for Decoration,' p. 4.

2. Give box one coat of VENETIAN RED in japan, thinned with turpentine, using a 1½ inch background brush. Allow to dry 24 hours.

3. Apply a second coat of VENETIAN RED. Allow to dry 24 hours.

4. Enlarge and apply the design according to instructions in Introduction, p. 5.

On the original box the circles were made with a sharp-pointed compass before the background paint was applied.

5. Paint the design according to color description below, using a No. 6 showcard brush or No. 3 quill for large designs and a No. 1 quill for dots.

DETAIL OF PENNSYLVANIA BOX—See Fig. 34

The spaces between the petals in the circles on the ends of the box are BLACK.

The petals are WHITE.

Large leaves on front of box, outer units of triangles at corners, and stems of tulips, DULL GREEN.

Center circles on left side of drawer, semicircles around handle, and first two leaves at each end, DULL GREEN.

Two outer semicircles on drawer, WHITE, other two BLACK.

Circle directly around knob on drawer, two center leaves on each side, and center circles on right side of drawer, BLACK.

Tulips on face of box, remaining circles, and center leaves on drawer, WHITE.

Heart design and center unit of triangles on all corners, CHROME YELLOW.

Band around large circles, and triangular units at corners, DULL GREEN.

The front panel has a ¼ inch stripe of CHROME YELLOW at each side, and at the ends a ½ inch stripe of BLACK. Bands and stripes are made with a striping quill.

The drawer has a ¼ inch stripe of DULL GREEN.

The rear upper corners have a ½ inch stripe around triangles of BLACK.

The black stripe on the front and the green leaves are outlined with dots of CHROME YELLOW.

The heart unit, yellow stripe, and white flowers are outlined with dots of BLACK.

Scallop on top of box has a ¼ inch CHROME YELLOW band. Base of scallop is ½ inch DULL GREEN stripe, under which are freehand brush strokes of CHROME YELLOW.

6. Allow the box to dry 24 hours, then apply one coat of varnish. After the varnish has dried 24 hours, antique according to directions for light backgrounds, p. 7.

7. Give two more coats of varnish 24 hours apart. Let dry 48 hours.

8. Rub with pumice and crude oil for a smooth finish.

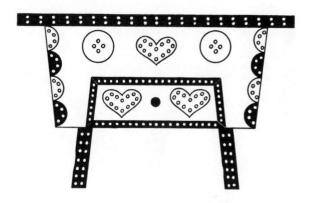

VENETIAN RED

DULL GREEN—chrome yellow medium, mixed with Prussian blue and a bit of raw umber.

CHROME YELLOW—chrome yellow medium toned with raw umber to mustard shade.

WHITE—flat white ready-mixed.

BLACK—flat black ready-mixed.

In addition to the materials listed under preparing wood for decoration, p. 4, and enlarging and transferring design, p. 5, you will need the following:

Materials	Where to buy	Amount
Paints:		
Flat black	Hardware store	½ pt.
Flat white	Hardware store	½ pt.
Chrome yellow medium		
in japan	Art supply store	1 tube
Prussian blue in oil	Art supply store	1 tube
Raw umber in oil	Art supply store	1 tube
Venetian red in japan	Art supply store	½ pt.
Brushes:		
1½" background	Art supply store	1
1½" varnish	Art supply store	1
No. 6 showcard or No.3		
quill	Art supply store	1
No. 1 small quill	Art supply store	1
No. 1 striping quill	Art supply store	1
Varnish	Art supply store	½ pt.
Powdered pumice	Hardware store	1 oz.
Turpentine	Hardware store	1 pt.
Crude oil	Art supply store	1 pt.
Compass	Art supply store	1

To Decorate Dough Trough Shown

1. Read instructions on how to prepare wood for decoration, p. 4.

2. The original trough shown is natural cherry (reddish-brown), unpainted. If you want to paint your trough, give it a coat of VENETIAN RED in japan, toned with raw umber to the desired shade. Allow to dry 24 hours.

3. Apply a second coat of the same color and allow to dry 24 hours.

4. Enlarge and apply the design according to instructions in Introduction, p. 5.

5. Paint the design, following color description below. Use a No. 6 showcard brush or a large quill brush for the larger units. For the small dots use a small quill brush held in a vertical position with just the tip touching. Read 'Freehand or Brush-stroke Painting,' p. 12.

Paint basic units first, planning to do all parts requiring the same color at one time, as it may be difficult to match the color later. Allow to dry thoroughly before applying dots.

Center of star and five dark points, DARK GREEN.

Tails of birds, remaining five points of star, and double circles in border around star, CHROME YELLOW.

Remaining circles in border, dark semicircles on base of trough, stripe on legs, and band around top, DARK GREEN.

Hearts on top of trough; large circles on upper part of base; light semicircles at edges of base; and heads, wings, and backs of birds, VERMILION.

Horse and hearts on base of trough, CHROME YELLOW.

Dots on yellow backgrounds, VERMILION.

Dots on vermilion and dark-green backgrounds, CHROME YELLOW.

6. Allow to dry 24 hours, then varnish. Let dry 24 hours.

7. Antique according to instructions for light background, p. 7.

8. Give two more coats of varnish 24 hours apart. Allow to dry 48 hours, then rub with pumice and crude oil.

COLOR GUIDE

VENETIAN RED

DARK GREEN—chrome green medium toned with raw umber.

CHROME YELLOW — chrome yellow medium toned with raw umber to mustard shade.

VERMILION

In addition to the materials listed under preparing wood for decoration, p. 4, and enlarging and transferring design, p. 5, you will need the following:

TOP OF DOUGH TROUGH—See Figs. 47 and 48

Materials	Where to buy	Amount
Paints:		
Venetian red in japan	Art supply store	½ pt.
Chrome yellow medium in japan	Art supply store	1 tube
Chrome green medium in japan	Art supply store	1 tube
Vermilion in japan	Art supply store	1 tube
Raw umber in oil	Art supply store	1 tube
Brushes:		
1¼″ background	Art supply store	1
No. 6 showcard or No. 3 large quill	Art supply store	1
No. 1 small quill	Art supply store	1
1½″ varnish	Art supply store	1
Varnish	Hardware store	½ pt.
Crude oil	Hardware store	½ pt.
Pumice	Hardware store	1 oz.
Turpentine	Hardware store	1 pt.

To Decorate Bucket Shown

1. Prepare bucket for decoration according to instructions on 'How to Prepare Wood for Decoration,' p. 4.

2. Paint outside of bucket DARK GREEN. Allow to dry 24 hours.

3. Paint inside of bucket WHITE, toned with raw umber.

4. Give outside of bucket second coat of DARK GREEN as described below. Allow to dry 24 hours.

5. Give hoops and handles a coat of flat BLACK. If necessary, give inside of bucket a second coat of WHITE. Allow to dry 24 hours.

6. Enlarge and apply the design according to instructions in Introduction, p. 5.

[45]

DETAIL OF WOODEN BUCKET—See Fig. 50

7. Paint the design, following color description below. Read description of brush-stroke painting, p. 12f.

Paint large base designs first, using No. 6 showcard brush or No. 3 quill, and allow to dry before adding fine lines and scrolls. These are done with a small quill and a No. 2 scroll brush. Plan your work to do all sections of a certain color at one time.

Large flowers, small flowers at top of design, and circular fruit, VERMILION.

Small three-petal leaves and light half of large leaves, CHROME YELLOW.

Leaves on hoops and dark half of large leaves, GREEN.

Stems, tendrils, and small brush strokes, VERMILION.

Fine lines in flowers and brush stroke on circular fruit, CHROME YELLOW.

Veinings on both yellow and green leaves,

LAMP BLACK.

Allow to dry 24 hours, then varnish.

8. Antique according to instructions for dark backgrounds, p. 7.

9. Give two more coats of varnish 24 hours apart.

COLOR GUIDE

DARK GREEN—pale-green flat oil paint tinted to the desired shade with Prussian blue and raw umber.

CHROME YELLOW — chrome yellow medium toned with raw umber to a mustard shade.

GREEN—either chrome green medium lightened with yellow and toned with raw umber, or a mixture of chrome yellow, Prussian blue, and a small amount of raw umber to obtain desired leaf-green color.

VERMILION

In addition to materials listed under preparing wood for decoration, p. 4, and enlarging and transferring design, p. 5, you will need the following materials:

On bellows a stencil design was often applied over the smoked marble background described under 'Two-toned Finishes,' p. 23.

To stencil on glass, the stencil is applied on the reverse side. The same technique is used as for stenciling on wood, but clear Serviseal is used instead of the regular varnish. Remember to place your stencil in reverse, so that when you turn the glass over, the design will be in the correct position.

To Stencil Frame Shown

1. Prepare surface for painting (see page 4).
2. Cut stencil in units as illustrated according to directions on p. 18.
3. Give frame two coats of flat black, thinned with turpentine if necessary, and allow to dry 24 hours between each coat.
4. Give frame a thin coat of varnish. Allow to dry to the sticky stage (read instructions on 'Applying the Design,' p. 20). Have ready the bronze powder you will need on your velour palette, and the silk velvet fitted to your finger.
5. To apply the stencil, center the eagle unit on top section of the frame and with pale-gold bronze powder rub gently over the stencil. These stencil designs should be quite bright and do not require shading. Using the cross-shaped unit, apply lengthwise to each side of the frame, allowing the crosspiece to run off the edges.

Center the same unit on the bottom piece of the frame and apply the bronze powder to the middle section, allowing the long ends to run off.

Repeat the star-medallion unit in each corner of this bottom piece.

Pale-gold bronze is used throughout.

6. Allow to dry 24 hours and apply a coat of varnish, to which a small amount of raw umber may be added to give an antique effect. Let dry 24 hours.
7. Apply two more coats of varnish, allowing 24 hours between each coat.
8. Allow the last coat to dry 48 hours, then rub with a mixture of powdered pumice and crude oil.

In addition to the materials listed under 'How to Prepare Wood for Decoration,' p. 4, 'Cutting the Stencil,' p. 18, and 'Applying the Design,' p. 20, you will need the following:

Materials	Where to buy	Amount
Paints:		
Chrome yellow medium in japan	Art supply store	1 tube
Raw umber in oil	Art supply store	1 tube
Chrome green medium in japan	Art supply store	1 tube
Prussian blue in oil	Art supply store	1 tube
Lamp black	Art supply store	1 tube
Vermilion in japan	Art supply store	1 tube
Flat white	Hardware store	½ pt.
Flat black	Hardware store	½ pt.
Flat pale-green	Hardware store	½ pt.
Brushes:		
No. 6 showcard or No. 3 large quill	Art supply store	1
No. 0 small quill	Art supply store	1
No. 2 scroll	Art supply store	1
1″ background	Art supply store	1
1″ varnish	Art supply store	1
Varnish	Hardware store	½ pt.

STENCILING

The same method of stenciling used for furniture was used on accessories—cornices, bellows, picture frames, mirrors, clocks, and clock and mirror glasses.

STENCILS FOR FRAME—See Fig. 68

Materials	Where to buy	Amount
Flat black paint	Hardware store	Small can
Pale-gold bronze powder	Art supply store	1 oz.
Raw umber in oil	Art supply store	1 tube
1⅛″ background brush	Art supply store	1
1⅛″ varnish brush	Art supply store	1
Varnish	Art supply store	½ pt.
Powdered pumice	Art supply store	1 oz.
Crude oil	Art supply store	½ pt.
Turpentine	Hardware store	½ pt.

TWO-TONED FINISHES

The finishes most often found on accessories such as picture frames, bellows, boxes, and small chests are graining, marbling, mottling, and finger painting, described under furniture finishes, p. 23.

GLASS PAINTING

Glass painting was used chiefly to decorate the panels of mirrors and clocks.

The process is not difficult for the amateur, but it takes time and care to insure delicate lines and even-flowing brush strokes.

This type of painting is done in reverse, the paint being applied to the inside of the glass. Highlights and shadows are painted in first and are backed by the various colors. The final step is a complete coat of opaque paint, usually a grayish white.

To Reproduce Glass Painting Shown

1. Be sure your glass fits the space it is to occupy. Wash with soap and water and then with a piece of cotton dipped in carbon tetrachloride. Do not touch or smear the glass with your fingers while applying the design.

2. Enlarge or reduce the design to the size of the glass, according to instructions in Introduction, p. 5. Then with a crow-quill pen and India ink, trace the design on transparent tracing paper. Place glass over the wrong side of the tracing paper and secure with scotch tape placed close to edge of glass. (It is also possible to trace outlines directly on right side of glass with pen and India ink, turning it to the reverse side for painting.)

3. Using a striping brush and flat black paint with a bit of varnish, put in a narrow black stripe, to frame the picture. Paint outlines and shadows of shell border with small quill and the black paint. The scallops may be done with either a scroll brush or a crow-quill pen, using black Serviseal thinned with a few drops of turpentine.

4. Prepare sizing liquid by dissolving one empty gelatin capsule in four ounces of very hot water. Apply it with large quill brush to the border, which is to be covered with gold leaf. Keep mixture warm.

5. Lift the gold leaf with wax paper (see p. 25), and apply it to the wet size. Stand the glass immediately so size can run off. Let dry.

6. Paint over the pattern with black Serviseal to hold the gold leaf. When it is dry, wipe off excess gold with damp cotton. Make sure the entire glass is clean.

7. Following picture pattern, trace all black outlines with flat black and a small amount of varnish, using a fine-pointed quill brush. Pattern in rug (dots and outline of stripes), all fine lines in baby's dress, flower centers, chair shadows, hair and dog fur, as well as face features, are also done in black with fine brush or pen.

8. You are now ready to apply colors according to the following color description, using tube oils and quill brushes, square-tipped ones for the larger areas and pointed small ones for details. Keep within outlines, remembering that the painting is in reverse and cannot be covered over. Any areas to be painted over must dry between coats.

Ruff on lady's collar and baby's hat, PINK.

Hands, arms, and faces, FLESH.

Hair, inside back of chair, and spotted seat of chair, BROWN.

Lady's dress and stockings, LIGHT GRAY.

Collars, cuffs, and shoes, shadows on lady's dress and cloak, DARK GRAY.

Lady's cloak and border top of footstool, YELLOW OCHRE.

Frame of chair, baby's dress, top and scallops of footstool, flowers, top border of floor pattern, RED.

Leaves, base of footstool, and vase, YELLOW OCHRE.

Dog, BROWN.

Squares in rug alternating RED and GREEN in horizontal rows.

Sky, shaded BLUE and PINK.

Stripes in rug, YELLOW OCHRE.

Note: For sky, mix white with a bit of alizarin crimson and umber to a very light pink, with a good amount of varnish. Start at bottom and fade into lighter tones of pink about level with chair top. Mix white with a bit of Prussian blue and a touch of umber, to obtain a very pale blue. Start this on top of pale pink and blend into deeper blue at top, adding more blue as needed.

Shadings are worked with paint thinned out with varnish in lighter sections.

Examine picture from other side frequently to see whether you are achieving the desired effect.

9. When paint is completely dry, apply backing of flat white toned with umber and thinned with turpentine. A second coat may be applied 24 hours later.

COLOR GUIDE

PINK—titan white mixed with alizarin crimson and touch of yellow ochre.

FLESH—titan white with bit of burnt sienna.

BROWN—burnt umber lightened with yellow ochre.

LIGHT GRAY—titan white with raw umber.

DARK GRAY—a bit of lamp black added to light-gray mixture.

RED—alizarin crimson lightened with white to a rosy hue.

GREEN—chrome yellow light, with Prussian blue and a bit of raw umber to obtain a green-leaf tint.

[49]

YELLOW OCHRE

In addition to materials listed under enlarging and transferring the design, p. 5, you will need the following:

Materials	Where to buy	Amount
Paints (in oil):		
Alizarin crimson	Art supply store	1 tube
Titan white	Art supply store	1 tube
Yellow ochre	Art supply store	1 tube
Burnt sienna	Art supply store	1 tube
Burnt umber	Art supply store	1 tube
Raw umber	Art supply store	1 tube
Lamp black	Art supply store	1 tube
Chrome yellow light	Art supply store	1 tube
Prussian blue	Art supply store	1 tube
Flat black	Hardware store	½ pt.
Flat white	Hardware store	½ pt.

Materials	Where to buy	Amount
Brushes:		
No. 3 large square-tipped quill	Art supply store	1
No. 0 fine-pointed quill	Art supply store	1
No. 2 scroll	Art supply store	1
No. 1 striping quill	Art supply store	1
Gold leaf (for glass)	Art supply store	1 book
Carbon tetrachloride	Art supply store	1 can
India ink	Art supply store	1 bottle
Crow-quill pen	Art supply store	1
Scotch tape	Art supply store	1 roll
Transparent tracing paper	Art supply store	1 pad
Empty gelatin capsule	Drug store	1
Glass	Hardware store	size of panel
Turpentine	Hardware store	1 pt.
Varnish	Hardware store	Small jar
Black Serviseal	Art supply store	½ pt.
Cotton	Drug store	1 pkg.

NEW ENGLAND GLASS PAINTING—See Fig. 60

34. PENNSYLVANIA BOX

35. PENNSYLVANIA DOUGH TROUGH

[51]

36. SPOON RACK

37. NEW ENGLAND CHEST

38, 39, 40. PENNSYLVANIA TRINKET BOX AND
DETAILS OF ENDS

41. PENNSYLVANIA CANDLE BOX

42. PENNSYLVANIA BOX

43. PENNSYLVANIA BOX

44. PENNSYLVANIA KNIFE BOX

45. PENNSYLVANIA BRIDE'S BOX

46. PENNSYLVANIA SALT BOX

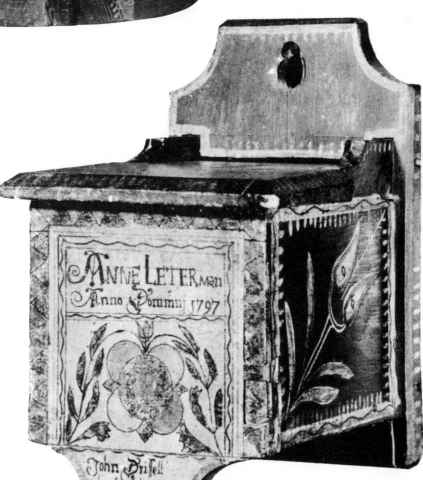

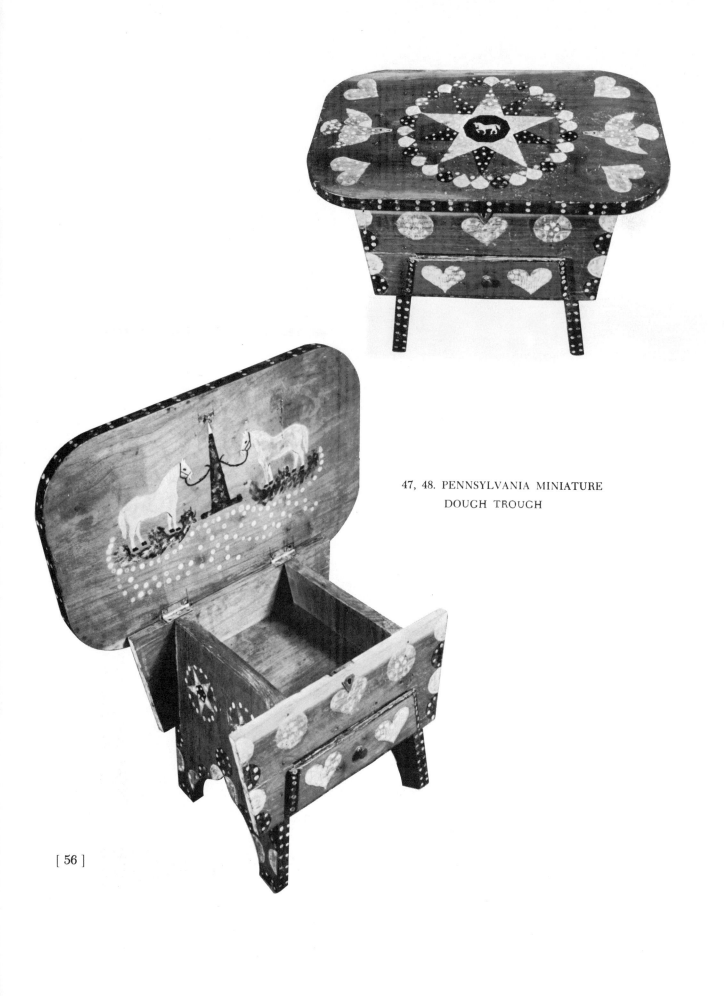

47, 48. PENNSYLVANIA MINIATURE
DOUGH TROUGH

49. PENNSYLVANIA SALT BOX

50. PENNSYLVANIA
WATER BUCKET

[57]

51. PENNSYLVANIA
SAFFRON CONTAINER

53. PENNSYLVANIA HEARTH BRUSH

52. PENNSYLVANIA SEWING STAND

54. PENNSYLVANIA COVERED PAIL

55. PENNSYLVANIA
CLOTHES BRUSH

[58]

56, 57. CORNICES FOR VENETIAN BLINDS FROM NEW YORK

58. NEW ENGLAND
PAPIER-MACHÉ TRAY [59]

59. CONNECTICUT SHELF CLOCK

60. NEW ENGLAND
    GLASS PAINTING

61. MIRROR
    GLASS PAINTING

62. EMPIRE-TYPE MIRROR

63. PENNSYLVANIA WAG-ON-THE-WALL CLOCK

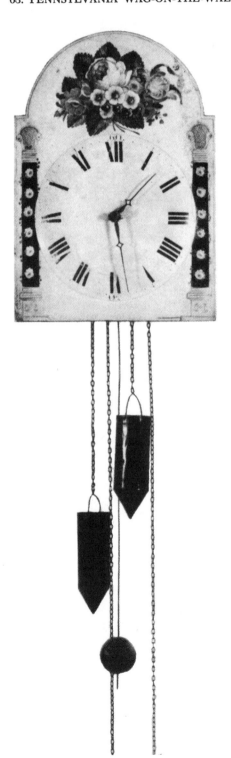

64. PENNSYLVANIA MIRROR

65. BELLOWS
FROM VERMONT

66. PENNSYLVANIA
PICTURE FRAME

67. PENNSYLVANIA PICTURE FRAME

[63]

68. NEW ENGLAND PICTURE FRAME

CHAPTER 3

ORNAMENTED TINWARE

Manufacture and Sale · Regional Characteristics

It will surprise many to find that American decorated tin originated in New England and not in Pennsylvania. In 1730 two Irish tinsmiths, William and Edgar Pattison, settled in Berlin, Connecticut. In 1740 they began importing sheet tin from England and making it into cooking utensils, which they sold from door to door in Berlin and neighboring towns. Soon Berlin became the center of the tin industry, which continued there till the middle of the ninetenth century.

The earliest tin was undecorated. By the late eighteenth century, however, tin was being 'japanned'—colored decoration applied over a lacquered ground—and one Hiram Mygatt, an 'ornamental coach painter,' opened a shop in Berlin for the japanning of tinware. Other tinware shops sprang up in Farmington and near-by Connecticut towns. In Boston, in 1785, Paul Revere advertised 'Japanned tea trays in sets,' and in 1799 Eli Parsons advertised his 'Tinning Business' in Dedham, Massachusetts. By then there were numerous tinsmiths operating in other New England communities.

The earliest American tinsmiths ornamented their tin in the manner of the 'japanned ware' that had been manufactured in England and Wales in the late seventeenth and eighteenth centuries. A great deal of this decorated tin was made in the eighteenth century for the American trade. In America the early tin was elaborately decorated by skilled workmen trained in the techniques used abroad. The eighteenth-century Chippendale and lace-edged trays painted with elegant floral designs, or decorated with gold-leaf or freehand bronze painting, are typical of this early period when tin decoration was patterned after English models. This kind of tin does not come into our folk category.

Soon, however, the rural tinsmiths began to turn out a type of simply painted tin intended for quick and cheap quantity sale. This country tin was made and decorated in enormous quantities in Pennsylvania in the first half of the nineteenth century, and has become popularly known as 'Pennsylvania tin.' It was also manufactured in German-settled communities outside Pennsylvania, such as the vicinity of Saugerties, New York. A great deal of the same type of tin also comes from New England.

While much of the nineteenth-century country tin was sold in stores—some was even given away as a premium with a packet of tea or a pound of coffee—more of it was peddled from carts. The first tin peddlers carried the light tinware on their backs in large tin trunks; later they traveled on horseback with their packs, and then in horse-drawn carts that were specially made with boxed bodies for storing the tin. Some of the tin peddlers bartered tin for farm produce, leaving home with a cart full of tin and returning with a load of supplies.

It was a great event when the tin peddler appeared on the village green and opened his packs. The women dropped their chores and the men their work to hear the gossip of the neighborhoods the peddlers had recently left. Everyone was eager to see the gaily decorated tinware that was so light to handle and made such a vivid bit of decoration. The peddler tried to time his [65] arrival for market days or military training days, when everyone was about. He always planned to come for the spring and autumn fairs, when people were in a holiday mood and would not mind spending the few pennies the tinware cost.

Richardson Wright in his *Hawkers and Walkers in Early America,* which is still the most authoritative book on the itinerants, describes the travels of the Connecticut tin peddlers:

'The early journeys of these peddlers' wagons were limited; then, as the countryside was opened up by more roads and by canals, the cart went farther and farther from its initial base of supplies. It was not unusual for them to cover 1200 to 1500 miles on a single trip, going down South, up to Canada, and westward through the interior. Practically every inhabited part of the United States was visited by them.

'The peddling trip generally began in late summer or winter. As the peddler went farther from his factory, his stock grew less. To keep him supplied the following method was devised by the home manufacturers. The tin workers at Berlin would pile up a large stock through the spring and summer months—five men working at home could keep twenty-five selling on the road. Then the tinsmiths would be sent to various towns in the South, where they would make up another supply and where a stock of general goods was kept on hand. These workers carried their tools and tinplate with them and traveled, where possible, by water. Richmond, New Bern, Charleston, Savannah, Albany, and Montreal were the usual points of temporary manufacture. Here the workers stayed through the winter. The peddlers always managed to route their journeys so that when they had finished their stock they were in the neighborhood of one of these towns. Here they handed their profits over to an agent and, re-supplied, started off on the road again for their spring and summer shifts. Then the workers returned to Connecticut. On the northern routes the peddlers started in early spring and the workers went to their temporary factories during the summer. As summer began, the wagons of the tin peddlers headed toward home. They usually foregathered in New York, where they sold their teams and wagons and went by boat back to Connecticut.'

This itinerant method of marketing tinware has complicated the problem of ascertaining its original source. Tin utensils have been found in all the towns where peddlers stopped, and people who do not know of the early itinerant sales methods naturally assume that the tin objects were made in the towns where they had been owned for close to a hundred years. Some of the Pennsylvania and Connecticut pieces that landed in other towns and states were doubtless imitated by local tinsmiths—which further confuses the issue. It is now generally thought that most of the decorated country tin we know originated in Pennsylvania, Connecticut, and Maine.

In Stevens Plains near Portland, Maine, Zachariah Stevens founded a large tin industry, whose products were marketed by peddlers throughout Maine and New Hampshire. The peddlers received about a dollar a day for their work. This Stevens Plains tinware was manufactured through the first half of the nineteenth century. It is distinguished by the use of a good deal of cream-white paint, either for the background or for the decoration. Figs. 72, 73, and 74 are typical examples.

In Connecticut Walter Goodrich (who subsequently moved to Stevens Plains), the Danforth family, and other tinsmiths decorated quantities of similar country tin.

A relatively small amount of tin is known to have been native to New York, though in Greenville a young lady named Ann Butler and her sisters, Marilla and Minerva, decorated and signed a good many pieces. This tin is of the Connecticut and Maine rather than the Pennsylvania type.

While there is great similarity in all this painted tin, the experts detect differences that enable them, tentatively at least, to separate the tin into groups of typical Pennsylvania and New England origin (see Figs. 69-94 for comparison). Even the tin manufactured in New York and other states was decorated in either the Pennsylvania or the New England manner. Earl Robacker and Titus Geesey, students of Pennsylvania tin, note a few basic differences of style that may help in identifying the place of manufacture, or at least the source of decoration. The Pennsylvania tin, Mr. Robacker states, is characterized by bolder use of color with fewer delicate tints and shades than one finds in pieces known to have been made in New England. The Connecticut tin, according to Mr. Geesey, also tended toward more detailed and less stylized designs than the typical Pennsylvania pieces. Pennsylvania tin appears gaudier, closer to the traditional German peasant decoration, which was part of the Pennsylvania German heritage.

The country tinsmiths decorated their tin with brush-stroke painting, which all the apprentice decorators learned. The colors used were white, yellow, blue, and vermilion on various-colored grounds, the commonest being black or brownish black. Other grounds are red, yellow, cream, blue, or green, the green being the rarest. The scarce red coffee pots were occasionally decorated in gilt. The designs, stylized as dictated by the brush-stroke technique, were most commonly made up of abstract patterns of fruits, flowers, and leaves. Some of the flowers are akin to the Adams rose of chinaware; fruits suggest the plum, tomato, and pomegranate. The decorated tin household objects were of many varieties—trays, sconces, tea caddies, tea and coffee pots, pitchers, measuring cups, salt shakers, nutmeg graters, hanging match cases, candlesticks, and many others. There were also boxes of various kinds, the commonest being cooky, spice, and trinket boxes, and the cash and document boxes that, according to Pennsylvania tradition, always accompanied the driver of the Conestoga wagon. Many of the tin pieces were made in miniature as toys for the children.

Gold and silver leaf was practically unknown to the country tinsmith, but after the 1820 period of furniture stenciling, tin decorators, too, learned the art of bronze stenciling and turned out many pieces decorated with simple stencil designs. The stenciled box and tray from Connecticut that we illustrate and describe in Figs. 98 and 103 and pp. 71-5 are good examples of the folk type of stenciled decoration.

Basic Instruction for Decorating Tin

PREPARING TIN FOR DECORATION

Old Tin

Remember to look for traces of old pattern before refinishing. Then remove paint with a paint remover, following directions on the can. If any rust spots appear, go over with a rust killer such as Rusticide, or any standard rust remover. Wash off all trace of the paint remover or rust remover with a cleaning fluid.

Now wash with hot water and soap, and dry thoroughly.

Immediately apply a coat of metal primer, such as red sanding primer. Thin with turpentine if necessary. Let dry 24 hours.

Rub with No. 00 waterproof sanding paper and water, until smooth.

Paint with a thin coat of flat black. Allow to dry 24 hours.

Sandpaper lightly with No. 00 waterproof sandpaper or No. 000 steel wool.

Give second coat of flat black. Allow to dry 24 hours and again sandpaper lightly.

Trays should be allowed to dry on one side before painting the reverse. They may be supported on four nails driven in blocks of wood if both sides must be done simultaneously.

Note: The beginner will find it easier to work with a black background, since any retouching done around the design on a black ground will not be visible after the varnish coat is applied.

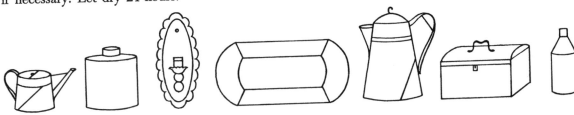

Always reserve enough paint from the original can for this retouching, so that the black will be the same. (All blacks do not match!)

For a light background follow directions above, using gray sanding primer. Tint flat white by mixing a little japan tube color, or artists' oil color, to the desired shade. A light background must have at least three coats of paint, allowing 24 hours to dry between each coat.

New Tin

Wash thoroughly with hot water and soap to remove any film of oil or grease. Rub with No. 0 coarse steel wool to roughen surface.

Give a priming coat of red primer, thinned with turpentine if necessary, and proceed as described above.

Materials	Where to buy	Amount
Paint remover	Paint store	1 can
Rust remover	Paint store	1 can
Metal primer	Paint store	1 can
Turpentine	Paint store	1 pt.
No. 00 waterproof sandpaper	Paint store	Several sheets
No. 000 and No. 0 steel wool	Paint store	1 pkg. each
Flat black paint	Paint store	½ pt.
Brush (for paint remover)	Paint store	1
1" brush (for background)	Paint store	1
Cleaning fluid	Paint store	1 can

BRUSH-STROKE PAINTING

Patterns and Colors

Very simple decorative patterns of leaves, flowers, and fruits were used. Commonest colors were vermilion, yellow, and green, on black or asphaltum grounds.

To Apply the Design

After the tin has been properly prepared as described in the preceding paragraphs, copy the design to be used on a piece of ordinary tracing paper.

Rub back of paper with a piece of magnesium carbonate for a dark background, or use black graphite paper for light backgrounds.

Place the tracing paper on the article to be decorated, holding in place with masking tape. Trace over the design with a No. 3 hard pencil.

To Paint the Design

See description of brush-stroke painting in chapter 1, p. 12, and practice on a piece of white paper the various brush strokes shown on p. 69.

To Decorate Coffin Tray Shown

1. Prepare tray for decoration as described on p. 67.

2. Give tray thin coat of flat black. (Background shown is brown asphaltum. It is a difficult medium to use and not recommended for the beginner.) Follow instructions under 'Preparing Tin for Decoration,' p. 67, for applying additional coats of paint.

3. Mark width of border on tray with pencil dots.

4. Paint the border background with flat white toned to a light gray with a bit of umber. Use a 1-inch background brush and keep within the pencil dots. Let dry 24 hours.

5. Enlarge and apply design to border according to instructions in the Introduction, p. 5.

6. To paint design use a large quill brush on large areas, smaller quill for buds, and scroll brush for fine lines and veins.

Paint all areas of one color at one time before proceeding to next color.

Paint all leaves GREEN.

When leaves are dry, paint side tulips, end buds, and center motif between leaves CHROME YELLOW.

End tulips, remaining buds and flowers, VERMILION.

When these are dry, put in all veins and fine lines and dots in LAMP BLACK.

Let dry 24 hours.

7. Using large quill, paint simple brush-stroke border on slanting edge CHROME YELLOW.

8. Apply coat of clear varnish to each side of tray. Let dry 24 hours.

9. Antique and apply at least five more coats of varnish as described on pp. 6 and 7.

10. Rub down with soft, lintless cloth, dipped in pumice and crude oil.

COLOR GUIDE

GREEN—chrome yellow medium mixed with Prussian blue and toned with raw umber to light green.

DETAIL OF TRAY—See Color Plate III, front cover

CHROME YELLOW — chrome yellow medium, toned with raw umber to mustard shade.

VERMILION.

In addition to materials listed under preparing tin for decoration, p. 68, and enlarging and transferring design, p. 5, you will need the following:

Materials	Where to buy	Amount
Paints:		
Flat black	Paint store	Small can
Flat white	Paint store	Small can
Raw umber in oil	Art supply store	1 tube
Prussian blue in oil	Art supply store	1 tube
Lamp black in oil	Art supply store	1 tube
Chrome yellow medium in japan	Art supply store	1 tube
Vermilion in japan	Art supply store	1 tube
Brushes:		
1″ background	Art supply store	1
No. 3 large quill	Art supply store	1
No. 1 small quill	Art supply store	1
No. 2 scroll	Art supply store	1
1½″ varnish	Art supply store	1
Varnish	Art supply store	Small can
Powdered pumice	Art supply store	1 oz.
Crude oil	Art supply store	1 oz.
Turpentine	Art supply store	1 pt.

To Decorate Cooky Box Shown

1. Prepare surface for painting as described on p. 67.

2. Apply thin coat of VERMILION in japan. Follow instructions for preparing tin for decoration, substituting vermilion for flat black.

3. Enlarge and transfer design according to instructions in Introduction, p. 5.

4. For painting, use large No. 3 quill for large areas and small No. 1 quill for small units. Use a No. 2 scroll brush for all fine lines. Be sure one unit is dry before adding overtones.

Paint birds YELLOW.

Center of light circle, two circular motifs, flower buds, and flowers, ROSE.

Central sections of pineapples at bottom, VER-MILION.

Let dry 24 hours.

5. Paint petals on flowers and centers on buds RED.

Stems, lighter leaves, and brush strokes at end of pineapples and on cover, YELLOW.

Let dry overnight.

6. Paint shadings on pineapples PINK. All dark circles, leaves, birds' wings, and outside of pine-apples, DARK GREEN. Small light dots and high-lights on circles and flowers, YELLOW. Eyes and all fine, dark markings on birds and circles, BLACK. Let dry 24 hours.

7. Apply coat of clear varnish and let dry 24 hours.

8. Antique according to instructions for light backgrounds, p. 7.

9. Apply two more coats of varnish 24 hours apart, and when the last coat has dried 48 hours, rub with crude oil and pumice.

COLOR GUIDE

CHROME YELLOW — chrome yellow medium toned to mustard shade with raw umber.

ROSE—alizarin crimson with a bit of titan white added for opacity.

PINK—titan white with alizarin crimson and bit of yellow ochre to pale shade.

RED—alizarin crimson.

DARK GREEN—chrome green medium with raw umber.

VERMILION

LAMP BLACK

In addition to materials listed under 'Preparing Tin for Decoration,' p. 68, and 'To Enlarge Design,' p. 5, you will need the following:

Materials	Where to buy	Amount
Paints:		
Vermilion in japan	Art supply store	1 tube
Chrome yellow medium in japan	Art supply store	1 tube
Raw umber in oil	Art supply store	1 tube
Alizarin crimson in oil	Art supply store	1 tube
Titan white in oil	Art supply store	1 tube
Yellow ochre in japan	Art supply store	1 tube
Chrome green medium in japan	Art supply store	1 tube
Lamp black in oil	Art supply store	1
Brushes:		
1" background	Art supply store	1
No. 3 large quill	Art supply store	1
No. 1 small quill	Art supply store	1
No. 2 scroll	Art supply store	1
1½" varnish	Art supply store	1
Powdered pumice	Art supply store	1 oz.
Crude oil	Art supply store	1 oz.
Varnish	Hardware store	½ pt.
Turpentine	Hardware store	½ pt.

STENCIL DECORATION

To stencil a tray or a box, the same directions apply as described in chapter 1 for furniture. Read carefully the instructions on 'Cutting the Stencil' and 'Applying the Design,' pp. 18 and 20.

Practice on a piece of black paper before at-tempting to decorate your tin. To a piece of ordi-nary shelf paper apply two coats of flat black paint. Allow to dry 24 hours between each coat, then follow instructions for applying the stencil.

To Decorate Stenciled Tray Shown

1. Prepare surface for painting, using rust re-mover if necessary, and following general in-structions on p. 67.

2. Apply two coats of flat black to each side of the tray, following instructions for 'Prepar-ing Tin for Decoration,' p. 67.

3. Meantime, copy the pattern, enlarging it to fit your tray, according to instructions on p. 5.

4. Cut stencil units as described on p. 18. The bird stencil used in border has all outside edges trimmed to give shape of bird, after center de-tails have been cut.

[71]

5. Apply thin coat of varnish to floor of tray. Allow to dry to the sticky stage (read p. 75). Get ready materials needed, as listed below. Place the bronze powders in proper position on a piece of velour. Wrap silk velvet around tip of finger.

6. Begin with main unit of cart and figures, and place the stencil in position on the tray. With aluminum powder, rub evenly and polish brightly all areas.

Place tree trunk in position and, with pale-gold bronze powder at top, shade with orange down one side, blending with statuary bronze toward the bottom.

Next the house is placed in position and stenciled in pale gold. Clouds of orange are applied to roof section and side of house.

The fence is done in statuary bronze. Bushes are placed as shown, in pale-gold bronze.

Using the tree unit and pale-gold bronze, repeat this design to fill in the background as indicated on tracing.

The castle and house on the hill are placed in position and stenciled with pale gold, very faintly, with touches of orange on roof and larg-est solid section of castle.

Clouds are applied by dipping velvet-wrapped finger in silver and using circular motion, add streaks of orange and pale gold to show sunset.

Shadows on lawn are applied with circular motion in the same manner; use orange and pale-gold bronze.

Let dry 24 hours, then wipe off any excess powder with damp cloth.

7. To apply color, look at illustration, Fig. 103, and follow dark areas. Place small amount of varnish in jar top and, using showcard brush No. 6, mix on wax-paper palette with transparent colors in oil to light tints. Use alizarin crimson for rose colors on dress and hat of figure at left, child's skirt, and belt on other figure. Prussian blue is used for collar of right-hand figure and overskirt of figure at left; leave apron silver, and use cadmium yellow for hair and dress of hatless figure. Mixing cadmium yellow, Prussian blue, and raw umber, color the cart and trees, and apply in broad strokes to lawn in foreground. Mix burnt sienna with varnish and apply very thinly for flesh tints. The spots on the dog are

cadmium yellow, burnt umber, and burnt sienna. Let dry 24 hours.

8. With vermilion in japan, thinned with turpentine and a bit of varnish, paint in cherries on cart and scale, as indicated, adding green leaves of chrome yellow medium mixed with Prussian blue. All these are done with a small quill brush. For cherries, hold brush in a vertical position and just touch the design, using enough pressure to produce circle of desired size.

Paint in facial features with small pointed quill, using lamp black mixed with varnish.

BORDER

1. Give border a thin coat of varnish. Allow to dry to the sticky stage.

2. Starting at center of long side and placing bird stencil in position, apply pale-gold powder, beginning at center of unit and brushing out

lightly to edge of tray and a little beyond outline, producing a silhouette. Repeat on other side of tray and at each corner.

3. Place the flower unit in position between birds, and stencil one flower with aluminum

STENCILS FOR TRAY—See Fig. 103

[73]

bronze and the rest of the unit with pale gold. Repeat for other flower units between birds.

4. At ends, place geometric unit at each side of handle hole and stencil with a mixture of pale gold and aluminum. Allow to dry overnight.

5. Wipe off with damp cloth and then apply color as described above, using alizarin crimson on small and large flowers stenciled in gold, and Prussian blue on silver flower. Apply a mixture of cadmium yellow, Prussian blue, and raw umber to leaves. Let dry 24 hours.

6. Varnish and let dry 24 hours.

7. Finish with ¼-inch gold band around floor of tray, using a mixture of pale-gold bronze powder and varnish. A narrow yellow stripe goes just inside this gold band and on each side of stenciled border. Read instructions for striping in Introduction, p. 6.

8. Antique and finish with varnish coats as described on pp. 7 and 75.

In addition to materials listed under 'To Enlarge Design,' p. 5, 'Cutting the Stencil,' p. 20, 'Applying the Design,' p. 21, and 'Preparing Tin for Decoration,' p. 68, you will need the following:

Materials	Where to buy	Amount
Colors (in oil):		
Alizarin crimson	Art supply store	1 tube
Prussian blue	Art supply store	1 tube
Cadmium yellow	Art supply store	1 tube
Raw umber	Art supply store	1 tube
Burnt sienna	Art supply store	1 tube
Burnt umber	Art supply store	1 tube
Lamp black	Art supply store	1 tube
Chrome yellow medium		
in japan	Art supply store	1 tube
Yellow ochre in japan	Art supply store	1 tube
Vermilion in japan	Art supply store	1 tube
Bronze powders:		
Aluminum	Art supply store	1 oz.
Pale gold	Art supply store	1 oz.
Orange	Art supply store	1 oz.
Copper or statuary	Art supply store	1 oz.
Silver	Art supply store	1 oz.
Flat black paint	Paint store	½ pt.
Brushes:		
Striper	Art supply store	1
No. 6 showcard	Art supply store	1
No. 0 small quill	Art supply store	1
No. 0 pointed quill	Art supply store	1
1½" varnish	Art supply store	1
Powdered pumice	Art supply store	1
Crude oil	Art supply store	½ pt.
Varnish	Art supply store	½ pt.

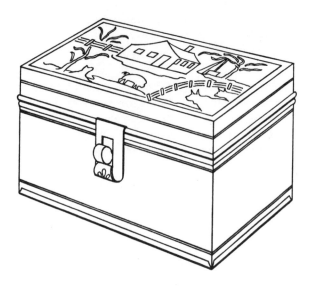

To Decorate Stenciled Box Shown

1. Prepare surface for painting. The original box had a transparent blue background. It is recommended that such a background be applied only to bright, shiny tin. If your box is new, or without blemishes, wash thoroughly and rub with No. 0 steel wool to remove any oily finish. Wipe carefully with Carbona. Pour enough varnish in a jar top to cover the surface, and mix in Prussian blue oil color to desired shade. Paint

STENCILS FOR BOX. See Figs. 98 and 99

with soft brush, avoiding streaks and bubbles. Let dry at least 24 hours.

If your box is old, it is advisable to use a black background. Follow instructions on 'Preparing Tin for Decoration,' p. 67.

2. Copy pattern and enlarge as described on p. 5.

3. Cut large and small stencil units according to directions on p. 18.

4. Give the box top a thin coat of varnish. Allow to dry to the sticky stage. Read instructions on stenciling, p. 20. Get ready the materials you will need, placing powders in small mounds on the velour palette.

5. Centering the stencil on top of the box, do the tree trunks, fences, side of house, and sheep, in pale gold. The pig and well are done in brass powder, the front of the house filled in with orange.

Make a tiny cornucopia of the velvet. Dip the tip in a mixture of orange and pale-gold powder. Draw across the lawn as indicated for shadows and puddles. The foliage is this same mixture, applied with the velvet wrapped around the finger and patted on to resemble leaf clusters. Lawn shadows may be filled in more fully this way if needed.

Allow to dry overnight. Wipe off with damp cloth.

6. With fine brush, paint in all windows and doors, using a bit of lamp black mixed with varnish. Allow to dry 24 hours.

7. Give a coat of varnish and allow to dry 24 hours.

8. Stripe around top and edge of box with toned yellow in japan, according to directions on striping, p. 6. Let dry overnight.

9. Apply two more coats of varnish, the first of which may contain a small bit of raw umber to dull the bright gold. Apply the second coat clear.

10. Allow to dry 48 hours, and then rub with a mixture of powdered pumice and crude oil.

In addition to materials listed under 'To Enlarge Design,' p. 5, 'Cutting the Stencil,' p. 20, 'Applying the Design,' p. 21, and 'Preparing Tin for Decoration,' p. 68, you will need the following:

Materials	Where to buy	Amount
Paints:		
Flat black *or*	Paint store	½ pt.
Prussian blue in oil	Art supply store	1 tube
Chrome yellow medium		
in japan	Art supply store	1 tube
Yellow ochre in japan	Art supply store	1 tube
Raw umber in oil	Art supply store	1 tube
Lamp black in oil	Art supply store	1 tube
Bronze powders:		
Orange	Art supply store	1 oz.
Pale gold	Art supply store	1 oz.
Brass or brilliant rich		
gold	Art supply store	1 oz.
Brushes:		
No. 1 small quill	Art supply store	1
No. 1 striping quill	Art supply store	1
1″ varnish	Art supply store	1
Powdered pumice	Art supply store	1 oz.
Crude oil	Art supply store	½ pt.
Varnish	Art supply store	½ pt.

GOLD-LEAF DECORATION AND FREEHAND BRONZE PAINTING

Read directions in chapter on furniture, p. 25. These techniques are characteristic of elaborate rather than simple folk styles of decoration. They are not recommended for amateurs.

FINISHING TIN

Striping

Read directions for striping in Introduction, p. 6.

Varnishing

Read carefully the directions on varnishing in Introduction, p. 6.

Before applying varnish to your tray or other piece of tin, wash the piece well with soapy water, then rinse thoroughly, and dry with a silk stocking or other lintless cloth.

Have your piece of tin slightly warm, and the varnish at room temperature.

Always keep your tray flat when varnishing, and also while it is drying.

For a smooth, satiny finish your tray will need at least six coats of varnish. Allow at least 24 hours to dry between each coat. Raw umber may be added to the first two coats to antique.

After the third coat, rub gently with No. 00 sandpaper, No. 000 steel wool, or fine powdered pumice and water. To use the pumice and water, place a small amount of pumice on a piece of newspaper. Take a piece of soft cloth, dip first in water and then in pumice, and rub gently on the tray. Rinse under running water to remove loose particles. Dry thoroughly.

Sandpaper or rub down after each subsequent coat of varnish.

When the last coat of varnish has dried (at least 48 hours), rub gently with crude oil and pumice. Use plenty of oil. Wipe off the oil and pumice with a clean, soft cloth.

To make a tray alcohol-proof, best-quality spar varnish is used for the last coat.

COMMON TYPES OF TRAYS

More people are interested in decorating trays than any other kind of tin. It is advisable to know the proper kind of design for the type of tray you plan to decorate. The eighteenth-century trays were not decorated in the native folk style that is explained in this book.

Lace-Edge Trays—made in the eighteenth century. They were round, oval, or rectangular in shape. The decoration was flowers or fruit as a central motif, surrounded by small sprays, with a fine gold-leaf border at the edge. A conventional urn was also used as a central motif. The background was usually 'tortoise shell' finish.

Gallery Trays—made about the same time as the Lace Edge. They were oval in shape, some with a solid standing edge, others with a pierced edge. The decoration was often similar to the Lace Edge, though many had landscapes or medallion portraits.

Chippendale, Gothic, or Pie-Crust Trays—appeared in the late eighteenth century. They were usually decorated with a gold-leaf scroll border on black, green, dark blue, or bronze backgrounds. Some had simple floral sprays at the edge with an undecorated center. Others had an elaborate decoration on the face of the tray—painted birds, flowers, and fountains, further decorated with gold and silver leaf with an overlay of brilliant color.

Rectangular Trays—made in the late eighteenth and nineteenth centuries. They had stenciled or freehand bronze and gold-leaf borders two to three inches wide, sometimes with the center left undecorated. Many had an elaborate freehand painting or a stenciled decoration of fruits and flowers on the face of the tray. Some were done with a landscape decoration. Later rectangular trays were stenciled with designs such as the one we describe on p. 71.

Octagonal Trays—made about the same time as the rectangular trays. The earlier ones were decorated with flowers, fruit, and leaves, in a simple gold-leaf border. Later they carried a stenciled border and a landscape or medallion in the center.

Oval or Windsor Trays—popular during the Victorian era. They were decorated with a large variety of designs. Many were used in inns and taverns, and they often carried a design showing the entrance to an inn, or a horse and rider. Some had elabrate floral decorations.

Coffin Trays—small country tin trays made in quantities in the nineteenth century, in the shape of the old eight-sided coffin. They had either flat-black or asphaltum backgrounds. The face was often painted with a wide white band with a conventional border of fruit and flowers done in red and yellow, with green leaves, and, around the edge, a yellow brush-stroke border. The example described on p. 68 is typical.

Apple and Bread Trays—commonly used in the nineteenth century. They were usually painted black with a stenciled design. Some of the rectangular bread trays had conventional flower and fruit decoration done freehand. The apple trays are distinguished by the deep flaring sides.

69

69, 70, 71. CONNECTICUT TINWARE

71

70

74

72

72, 73, 74. MAINE TINWARE

73

[77]

75

76.

77

78

79

80

82

81

75-82. PENNSYLVANIA TINWARE

83-94. PENNSYLVANIA TINWARE

95. PENNSYLVANIA COOKY BOX

96, 97. PENNSYLVANIA COFFEE POTS

98, 99. NEW ENGLAND BOX AND DETAIL OF TOP

100, 101, 102. PENNSYLVANIA TRAYS

103, 104. NEW ENGLAND TRAYS

CHAPTER 4

STENCILED AND PAINTED FABRICS

Origin and Early Use · Possible Uses Today

One of the earliest forms of interior decoration, now scarcely remembered, was the painting of 'floorcloths' in various patterns and colors. Though only scraps of these painted carpets have been preserved, they may be observed in numerous paintings of the period (see Figs. 105-8) and we can tell how striking and vivid they were in the early rooms.

The very first floor covering used in America was a heavy, coated sailcloth painted in patterns, which covered the entire floor. In the seventeenth century, from as early as about 1650, these floorcloths were painted in tile-like designs. The contrasting blocks of color—dark red and yellow in one example, but most often black and white—were sometimes solid, sometimes marbleized.

By the eighteenth century the geometrical patterns were being replaced by freer and more elaborate designs, with a much greater variety of colors. Floorcloths are advertised in New York, Philadelphia, and Boston papers after 1720, but were evidently at their peak from the middle to the end of the century, when numerous advertisements bear witness to their popularity. An item in a Newburyport paper dated 1747 reads: 'Painted Canvass at Great Bargains. A large assortment of Painted Carpetings, comprising many styles and qualities at prices which cannot fail to give satisfaction. S. Sweetser & Sons, 5 Liberty St.' A *Boston News-Letter* of the late 1760's carries the typical advertisement of a John Gore, who announces 'Coach & Carpet Painting done in the best and cheapest manner,' and at about the same time one George Killcup advertises

that he 'Paints Carpets & other articles.' At this time painted carpets were also imported from London, as evidenced by a number of old bills for imported floorcloths. The painted carpets, manufactured in quantity in America from about 1750, were adapted from designs that were developed in England before 1650. The late eighteenth-century American floorcloths, with their elaborately designed repeat patterns, may be seen in numerous paintings by Gilbert Stuart, Edward Savage, and Ralph Earl.

By the nineteenth century the carpet patterns were generally stenciled rather than painted, and the method by which they were done is described by Rufus Porter in a little book called *Curious Arts,* published in Concord, New Hampshire, in 1825 (quoted, p. 86). The inclusion of these directions in Porter's popular instruction booklet indicates that carpet painting was at least fairly common in New England in the early nineteenth century. Some of these stenciled carpets may perhaps be identified in the provincial paintings of the period, though it is difficult to distinguish between stenciled and woven carpets in painted representations. Carl Dreppard, author of numerous books on antiques, reports that in Pennsylvania, as late as 1890, old rag carpets were rejuvenated by being coated with filler and several layers of paint, and were then decorated with bright tulip, leaf, and geometrical designs.

The painted carpets, which were used as part of the decorative scheme of American homes for over two hundred years, might be adapted for contemporary use in several ways. The reverse side of worn broadloom carpets, less likely to crack than filled rag carpets, could be properly surfaced and decorated as they were in Pennsylvania, with freehand Pennsylvania German designs painted on them to make a child's room or a den gay and colorful with minimum trouble and expense. The earlier New England designs could also be economically painted or stenciled on these carpets or on coated canvas. Authentic floor covering for a seventeenth- or eighteenth-century type of house, in which the universally used nineteenth-century hooked rugs are actually an anachronism, could easily be patterned after the simple geometrical designs of the old floorcloths. This would be especially desirable for shops and museums that habitually display early American furniture on modern hardwood floors.

The most engaging of the decorated fabrics used in the early homes were the stenciled bed hangings, counterpanes, and small table cloths. In these pieces brightly colored designs were applied with stencils on homespun cotton. In some examples the major decoration was stenciled and afterward various parts were touched up freehand. Though these stenciled cottons are now rare collectors' items, they were in everyday use little more than a hundred years ago. Several examples have come from Connecticut and Vermont and more from New York state. All were made around 1825, the period when theorem or stencil painting in watercolor and on velvet was generally taught as part of the curriculum in young ladies' seminaries. It seems likely that these counterpanes, fashionable in rural neighborhoods as substitutes for more elaborate embroidered spreads, were customarily made at home by the ladies of the family. Many of them are stenciled in green, yellow, blue, and red, the colors most commonly used for the theorem painting of the period. The vases of flowers in the counterpane found in Lisle, New York (Fig. 111), are very much like the primitive watercolor and velvet still-life paintings.

The old patterns stenciled on cotton bedspreads are among the most pleasing of our early American designs. It seems a pity that they are not popularly reproduced, though candlewick, patchwork, and crocheted bedspreads have been made by the thousands. Any of the lovely old stencil designs can easily be applied to a cotton spread with fabric colors designed to be safely cleaned or washed, and a bed decorated in this lively, primitive style would be a focus of interest in an early American bedroom. These designs might be stenciled as all-over patterns for bedspreads or table covers, or as running borders for tablecloths or luncheon sets, while a single unit such as one of the vases of flowers would be a jaunty bit of decoration for cocktail napkins, guest towels, or gift handkerchiefs, or for the decoration of the patch pocket on an apron.

Painted window shades were another form of early interior decoration that has been largely ignored. They were manufactured as early as the 1830's in the East, and by the 1840's in the Middle West as well. They were popular through 1860. A manufacturer of wallpapers tells that in the mid-nineteenth century his great-grandfather traveled by steamboat up and down the Ohio and Mississippi rivers, selling painted window shades. This indicates that the shades, like many of the items of folk art and decoration, were sold by itinerant peddlers.

Made usually in matching pairs or sets, the shades were sold ready-made and were also made to order with appropriate designs for steamboats, shops, and even undertakers. The ordinary painted decoration featured floral bouquets, fancy and landscape borders, Gothic windows, various Indian representations, and romantic and Oriental landscapes, which were the most popular subjects (see Fig. 113).

The majority of the shades were painted in transparent oil colors on thin muslin, and hung with the painted side toward the windows so that the decoration was visible from the outside and made a striking effect when the light shone through it into the room. The shades were turned out in quantity with the help of model patterns, and the quick, bold, shade-painting technique seems to have been as standardized a process as were stenciling methods for furniture and brush-stroke painting for tinware. Though the designs of these shades were generally derivative and the painting done with labor-saving factory methods, the strong colors and slapdash vigor and assurance of execution give them a robust folk flavor.

There are many rooms in which elaborate window draperies or Venetian blinds are inappropriate, and for such interiors it would be interesting to reproduce some early painted shades to be used in combination with simple curtains for an original and authentic window treatment.

The old practices of decorating carpets, stenciling cotton, and painting window shades need not be lost arts.

How to Decorate Fabrics

PAINTED AND STENCILED CARPETS

Painted floorcloths were popular in the eighteenth century and were still used during the nineteenth century.

Carl Dreppard, in an article written for *Town & Country*, describes floorcloths as follows: 'sailcloth, built up by application of a starch filler on both sides of the canvas, and then painted in patterns.'

He recommends modern linoleum inlay floors for seventeenth- and eighteenth-century interiors, done in the geometric patterns of the early floor carpets, which were painted in checkered or diapered patterns, imitating the marble floors of the Renaissance.

Rufus Porter, in his book, *Curious Arts*, published in 1825, describes carpets as follows: 'To paint in figures for carpets or borders: Take a sheet of pasteboard or strong paper, and paint thereon with a pencil, any flower or figure that would be elegant for a border or carpet figure; then with small gouges and chisels, or a sharp pen knife, cut out the figure completely, that it be represented by apertures cut through the paper. Lay this pattern on the ground intended to receive the figure, whether a floor or painted cloth, and with a stiff smooth brush, paint with a quick vibrative motion over the whole figure. Then take up the paper and you will have an entire figure on the ground.'

STENCILED FABRICS

To Prepare Material for Stenciling

Wash fabric with soap and water to remove sizing usually found in new cloth. Rinse thoroughly and press. Cotton was used for the early stenciled patterns and is practical for stenciling.

To Cut Stencil

FOR A ONE-COLOR STENCIL. Trace design carefully on a piece of transparent tracing paper with India ink and a fine quill pen, being careful to keep lines even and accurate.

Place the stencil paper over the tracing paper and retrace with a hard pencil.

Lay stencil over a piece of window glass and cut design with an Exacto knife.

FOR A DESIGN WITH MORE THAN ONE COLOR. Trace design as described above.

Using a separate piece of stencil paper for each color, retrace the individual color units.

FLOORCLOTH—Illustration from *Jane and Eliza*, 1840. Courtesy Carl Drepperd

An easy way to line up the units accurately is to take two pieces of adhesive tape and make a right angle to use as a guide. Fit each piece of stencil paper so that the left-hand corner fits into this guide. For a border, use a strip of cardboard as a guide.

Place stencils together and hold up to light to be sure the units of the design are in the correct place. Cut as described above.

[86]

Colors

Use textile colors, such as Prang, available at most paint stores or artists' supply stores.

Read carefully the directions that come with the colors.

Add Extendor (Prang) to all colors so that the color will penetrate the fabric better.

To make a color lighter, use more Extendor.

To make a color darker, add a bit of black.

TO APPLY THE COLOR. Place a piece of white blotter under the fabric.

Stretch the fabric across a drawing board and fasten securely with thumb tacks.

Work color into the brush and draw across a piece of paper or waste cloth to remove excess color.

Use a very small amount of color on your brush at a time. Several light applications are better than one heavy one.

Place stencil in position.

Apply color by placing brush on stencil about ½ inch from the edge of the design and drawing it across the opening toward the center.

Repeat until you have the desired color.

Work color well into the fabric. Never pile it on.

TO SET THE COLOR. Allow finished work to dry thoroughly, at least 24 hours. Colors may seem dry in a few minutes, but allowing them to set for at least 24 hours will insure a greater fastness of color.

When piece is thoroughly dry, place a cloth over the face of the design and iron for at least one minute with a hot iron, 350° F. Turn over and repeat on the other side. For rayon use a warm iron, 200° to 230° F., and iron for a longer period.

To Reproduce Stenciled Cotton Shown

1. Prepare the materials for stenciling as described, p. 86.

2. Enlarge design to fit fabric according to instructions, p. 5. Trace onto thin tracing paper.

3. Cut stencil units as instructed, p. 86, one for each color unit.

4. Fasten fabric onto board and prepare for stenciling (see p. 86). Assemble materials, colors, Extendor, and brushes. Read instructions that come with stenciling kit.

5. Using a No. 1 textile brush apply small amounts of colors at a time, following color description below and using stencil units as shown.

MOTIF NO. 1

Central circular unit and dotted loops, GREEN.

Petals (fringe and center), daisies, and lines at point of loops, ROSE.

STENCILS FOR FABRIC—See Fig. 112

Center of circular unit, ROSE; use portion of same stencil unit as leaf center below.

Center of daisies, YELLOW, with GREEN dot.

MOTIF NO. 2

Small flower in exact center and heart centers, YELLOW.

Leaf unit and dotted loops, ROSE.

Seaweed and dot in center, GREEN.

Daisies, YELLOW.

Daisy centers, ROSE, with GREEN dot.

Circles at loop points are painted GREEN, and hearts are outlined in ROSE freehand with small pointed brush.

Let dry 24 hours.

6. Set the color according to directions, p. 87.

Materials needed	Where to buy	Amount
Textile colors—red, green, yellow, black	Art supply store	1 jar
Extendor	Art supply store	1 jar
No. 1 textile brush	Art supply store	1
Small pointed brush	Art supply store	1
White blotter	Art supply store	1
Stencil paper	Art supply store	1 pad
Tracing paper	Art supply store	1 pad
India ink	Art supply store	1 bottle
Crow-quill pen	Art supply store	1
No. 11 or No. 16 Exacto knife	Art supply store	1
Drawing board	Art supply store	1
Thumb tacks	Art supply store	1 box
Window glass	Hardware store	Size of stencil

PAINTED WINDOW SHADES

Window shades were painted on fine-textured muslin. The muslin was stretched, given two coats of size, and then rubbed with pumice stone to smooth. It is believed that in the shops there was a master pattern, hung where all could see, and that the window shades were given to the workers with just the outline of the scene drawn in.

The outline of the design was applied by freehand copying, tracing, stenciling, or pouncing. In pouncing, perforated outlines were made on paper patterns and then transferred to the muslin by dusting the pricked-out design with a pounce bag containing pulverized charcoal. The pounced design of dotted lines was then drawn in India ink. After the design was outlined on the cloth, it was painted in transparent oil colors, mixed with japanners' gold size and turpentine so that it would set quickly and not run. White and opaque colors were avoided, as the light could not shine through them. Prussian blue, burnt sienna, and various greens and yellows were the most frequently used colors. In painting landscapes a soft sponge was often used instead of a brush for skies, and a coarse sponge for dabbing on the background color of the foliage.

Any cloth window shade can be easily painted in this manner. If it is an old shade, it must first be washed with soap and water to remove dirt and grease. Let dry thoroughly and then spread the shade on the floor or on a long table. Outline the design, and then paint with tube oil colors, thinned with turpentine, following the old methods as described above. Use large design brushes, imitating the stylized type of brushwork, which can be studied in Fig. 113; and if you wish, experiment with sponges for applying color to sky and foliage.

105

106

107

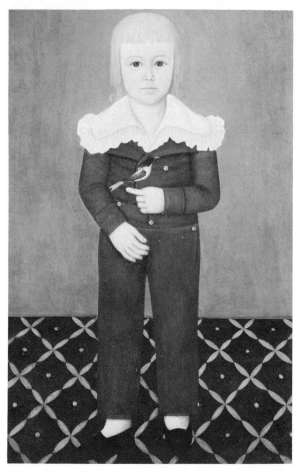

108

105-108. FLOORCLOTHS IN EARLY PAINTINGS

109. STENCILED COUNTERPANE

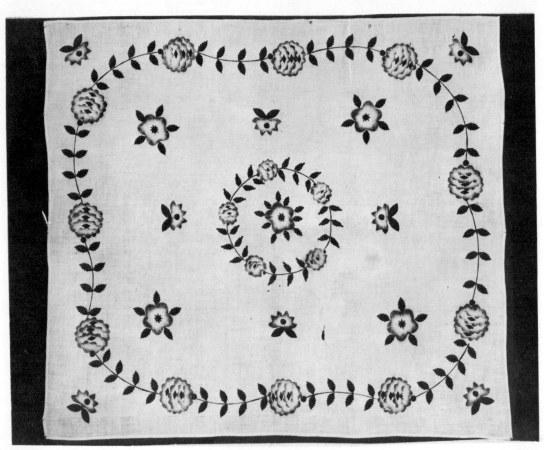

110. STENCILED
TABLE CLOTH

111. STENCILED COUNTERPANE
FROM NEW YORK

[92]

112. PORTION OF STENCILED COUNTERPANE FROM CONNECTICUT

113. PAINTED WINDOW SHADE
FROM NEW YORK

CHAPTER 5

ARCHITECTURAL DECORATION

Early House Painting · Pennsylvania Barns

The interior of the home of a certain Moses Morse of Loudon, New Hampshire, was portrayed in 1824 by a primitive painter named Joseph Warren Leavitt. The small watercolor (Fig. 114) is a delightful contemporary record of the way a New England room looked in the first quarter of the nineteenth century. Few such interiors retain their old decoration today, so not many people realize how very gay and colorful early American rooms could, and should, be.

The ivory-colored plaster walls in the picture are stenciled with borders of red and blue, and a large stenciled bird perched on a branch is featured as the overmantel decoration. The walls in the end room appear to be covered with an all-over stencil pattern. The woodwork is painted deep rose with ivory trim. The floor could be covered with a painted floorcloth, but in this case the floor itself seems to be painted, in squares of blue and buff. The walls, woodwork, and floors were very likely painted by the same decorator. He may have been one of the many itinerant house painters who, passing through Loudon, stopped at Mr. Morse's farmhouse long enough to do a complete redecorating job, getting as pay nothing more than the customary bed and board while he worked. It seems entirely possible that the decorator was Mr. Leavitt of Chichester, New Hampshire, the painter of the watercolor, who certainly featured the details of the interior decoration.

The stenciling and painting of plaster walls was an art that originated and developed in the rural districts of New England as a substitute for the expensive patterned and scenic wallpapers that came into style around 1790. Wallpaper, first imported from France and England and then manufactured here, was a luxury relatively few could afford. However, there was more leisure and desire for luxuries in the latter half of the eighteenth century, as well as increasing contact between communities. This resulted in the widespread desire for the painted interior decoration, which brought into rural homes the kind of color and design that the fashionable wallpapers had introduced into city mansions.

Plaster walls were decorated first with freehand and then with stenciled designs but not till later with landscapes, which were not common until the second quarter of the nineteenth century. Most of the walls were stenciled rather than painted freehand. The majority of these were done in the first quarter of the century.

Both patterned and landscaped walls originated in and flourished throughout New England, and then spread to New York and as far west as Ohio and Kentucky, where a number of stenciled walls have been found in towns that were settled by New Englanders.

Both the vogue for stenciled walls and the actual designs were carried from village to village by the journeymen decorators, who came on horseback with their simple materials and tools—dry colors, brushes, stiff paper or leather stencils, a measure, and builders' cord and a piece of chalk for spacing. All these were packed in a box that would fit across a saddle. The skimmed milk that was used as a medium for mixing the colors was obtained at each of the farms where the decorator stopped to work.

One of the itinerants discussed by Janet Waring, author of *Early American Stencils*, is Moses Eaton of Hancock and Dublin, New Hampshire. His kit of wall stencils and brushes, found in the attic of his house at Dublin, contained seventy-eight stencils, which made forty complete designs. The colors he used—red, green, and yellow—can still be seen on the old stencils, which are now owned by the Society for the Preservation of New England Antiquities in Boston. The stenciled walls that we reproduce as Figs. 128 and 130 are his.

The walls of houses and taverns were sometimes stenciled by local artisans as well as by itinerants, and occasionally by 'home talent.' A farmer's wife, named Lydia Eldredge Williams, decorated five rooms of her house in Ashfield, Massachusetts, about 1820; and about 1840 a Lucinda Pomroy is said to have stenciled the living room of her father's house in Somers, Connecticut (Fig. 131).

The ordinary colors used for wall stencils were reds, greens, yellow, and black, in various combinations, applied on white, pink, yellow, gray, light-green, or light-blue painted plaster. The color stenciled on the wall was always flat, never shaded. The pigments were made from natural powdered products, such as the local red, green, and yellow earth clays, and brick dust, mixed in skimmed milk. The white for the walls was simple whitewash, sometimes tinted with color; the black was lamp black, occasionally diluted with rum and water.

The most popular stencil motifs were conventionalized leaf and flower forms and geometric figures, and also festoons with tassels or bells for borders. The overmantel carried the elaborate pattern of the room, sometimes an eagle, peacocks, horsemen, weeping willows, or a basket of flowers. Many of the designs were repeated, for the itinerants traveled far and they frequently copied one another. Some motifs survived throughout the first quarter of the nineteenth century, and the same designs are found from Maine to New York and Connecticut to Ohio.

The placement of the patterns is generally similar to that of the conventional wallpapers, and the use of friezes, borders, and pilasters to break the surfaces into interesting spaces is

derived from wallpaper designs. The designs of the wallpapers dictated the basic arrangement of the stenciling on walls, but the actual designs were very slightly imitated. Stenciled walls have a decorative tradition of their own in America. The stencil, as a tool, conditioned the type of design, for intricate patterns were difficult and ineffectual. The stencil artists invented suitable designs or drastically simplified the patterns they found on wallpaper, carved woodwork, and carved and painted furniture.

As in other forms of early American decoration, there is some symbolism in these stencil designs. Hearts and bells suggested joy, the eagle was the emblem of liberty, the pineapple is recorded as denoting hospitality, willows suggested immortality. However, the ornamental interest was primary; and the essential characteristic of all stencil decoration is clarity and simplicity of color and design.

Landscape painting on plaster walls, popular in New England throughout the second quarter of the nineteenth century, is one of the most remarkable forms of early decoration, and the most interesting mural art produced in America. Rufus Porter (1792-1884), whom we have mentioned as author of a popular art-instruction book, was the outstanding wall painter of his time. He was also a typical Yankee Jack-of-all-trades. As a lad he left the family farm in Boxford, Massachusetts, and traveled on foot to Maine, where he earned his livelihood for several years as a drummer and drum painter, itinerant fiddler, house and sign painter, and schoolteacher. Later he became a dancing master, and then took to the road again as a silhouette cutter, portrait painter, and wall decorator. He was a well-known inventor as well, originating among scores of things the elevated railroad and an 'aerial locomotive'; and as a journalist he founded and edited the *New York Mechanic* and the still authoritative *Scientific American*.

Nearly a hundred of the houses Porter and a group of his followers decorated in Maine, New Hampshire, and Massachusetts survive today with many of the frescoes in fine condition, as may be seen in our selection of plates (Figs. 132-7).

Porter's landscape-painting technique, which he practiced through the second quarter of the nineteenth century, is first described in an item in his *Curious Arts* in 1825. In 1841 he published an art-instruction serial on 'Landscape Painting on Walls of Rooms' in the *New York Mechanic*, which he owned and edited, and in 1846 he presented this subject in final form in seven articles published in his *Scientific American*. Excerpts from these articles with some of the original illustrations are reprinted on pp. 103 and 104.

The articles on wall painting are part of a series planned to instruct the nineteenth-century public in all branches of painting—portrait and landscape painting as well as ornamental painting on glass, signs, carriages, window shades, and walls. Porter thought of wall painting as a practical form of decoration rather than as a fine art. He intended his instruction for the amateur painters of his time; and his methods could be followed today by the Sunday painters who would like to try landscaping instead of papering a room.

Porter states that the four walls of a parlor can be completely painted in watercolors in less than five hours, and at a total cost of ten dollars. In order to make possible this rapid technique, the content of the painting and the drawing and coloring were reduced to the simplest possible terms. The frescoes were executed in large scale in a combination of freehand painting and stenciling, some in full color, others in gray or plum or gray-green monochrome, with foliage sometimes rapidly stamped in with a cork stopper instead of being painted with a brush. These labor-saving methods had been used for decorating plaster, woodwork, and furniture, and Porter popularized them for landscape painting. His deliberately stylized landscapes, and those by his pupils, such as the one seen in Fig. 137, are so modern in spirit that they remind one of the work of Grant Wood and other twentieth-century painters of the American scene.

Porter always thought of his landscapes as simple wall decorations. His was a true folk art, original and unpretentious; it derived from craft rather than painters' traditions and aimed at solid, structural design rather than at academic realism or a fashionable, sophisticated style. The gray-monochrome landscapes in the old Winn house in Wakefield, Massachusetts (Figs. 135 and 136), give a good idea of Porter's typical plan for the decoration of a room. Notice especially the vertical emphasis of the paintings on the side walls, and the contrasting sweep of the over-mantel scene, with the two stenciled horsemen scooting over the exact center of the mantel.

Porter was not the first of the landscape decorators. The well-known Neapolitan, M. F. Cornè and other fine artists executed murals here a generation before Porter started landscaping walls. These murals were romantic, foreign-style landscapes designed, like the imported wallpapers, for the homes of wealthy merchants and landowners. There were also a few early wall painters who worked in a simple, native style.

Rufus Porter, however, was the first to popularize the everyday New England landscape as a subject for painting. He decorated walls, rapidly and cheaply, for the simple farmhouses and taverns of everyday folk, who could not afford expensive wallpaper or high-priced mural art. He worked as a unique itinerant decorator for the New England people of his time.

A specialized kind of wall decoration that should be mentioned was the ornamenting of Masonic meeting places with Masonic designs. On the east wall of the ballroom in the old Fuller Tavern in Berlin, Connecticut, there is a typical early Masonic picture painted in blue, green, brown, and red on a buff ground. The entire attic of a house in New Lebanon, New York, built by Elisha Gilbert, a Mason, is occupied by the old lodge room, which is covered with Masonic designs (Figs. 140, 141, and 142). These Masonic murals are said to have been done by a traveling wagon-painter Mason, who used ordinary wagon paint for the buff and brown designs and the sky-blue background. The Masonic room was completed about 1795, but the decorations appear to date from the early nineteenth century.

Woodwork, like plaster, was frequently painted in the early houses. In a house built about 1690 the whitewashed timbers were dotted with black in a spongework decoration, and sometimes timbers were ornamented with a crude zigzag pattern of black on white. After 1720 paint came into common use on woodwork, and in the early nineteenth century the sheathing was occasionally stenciled with simple patterns like those used for walls, and two-toned finishes and designs of various kinds were applied to paneling, molding, and doors.

In many houses and in some of the simple meeting houses of New England one still sees woodwork mottled to simulate marble, and panels grained to look like various rare woods. In some of the New England ship-building towns such as Kennebunkport in Maine, and Duxbury in Massachusetts, doors were grained by ship painters to look like the precious imported mahogany. The Jonathan Cogswell house in Essex, Massachusetts, built about 1740, contains several rooms with interesting painted woodwork, one of which is shown in Fig. 115. The panels are done in cedar rose with dark rose grained over the base coat of light pink. Other parts of the woodwork are marbleized in green and black. Different types of painted woodwork from New England and Pennsylvania are seen in the doors reproduced in Figs. 116 and 117.

In a few eighteenth-century houses a series of landscaped panels was a featured part of the woodwork, and in many the focus of the parlor decoration was a painted overmantel panel. The overmantel sometimes pictured the house or some part of the estate, as in Fig. 127, sometimes a local scene, as in Fig. 121, or an imaginary scene such as the landscape in Fig. 120. This, said to be a view of London, seems to combine elements of English, Italian, and New England architecture. Winthrop Chandler of Windham County, Connecticut, painted this overmantel panel. One of our outstanding eighteenth-century portrait painters, he was also one of the best painters of landscaped overmantels and fireboards.

A modern primitive-style panel painting of the house, like the one shown in Fig. 127, or a local view, such as we see in Fig. 121, would make an attractive overmantel feature for an early type of room. Such a painting could be executed by a professional artist, or, even better, by the owner himself. Primitives are so simply designed and painted that they are quite easy to imitate.

The fireboards, several examples of which are shown, were, like the overmantel panels, an interesting type of primitive painting used to add a decorative accent to early rooms. These fireboards, sometimes made of wood, sometimes of mounted canvas, were used to block off fireplaces during the summer season. They were generally decorated by the house painters who ornamented woodwork, floors, or walls, as was obviously the case in the Hibbard house in Ithaca, New York (Fig. 119). Edward Hicks, the well-known Quaker artist and preacher, who started his career as a house painter, made the Niagara Falls scene reproduced in Fig. 122 as a fireboard. Other fireboard subjects are seen in the anonymous paintings reproduced in Figs. 123-7.

Regardless of subject matter, there is a common denominator of style in these eighteenth- and nineteenth-century fireboard paintings. Style was dictated by function. Fireboards were intended as decorative pieces, meant to be seen clearly at some distance, from various parts of the room. The compositions were therefore simple, the outlines heavily painted, the colors flat and strong. Fireboards are among the most stylized of all the primitive paintings, and the boldest in color and design.

The floors of the early New England houses were one more important aspect of the decorative ensemble. In the earliest days, when floors were sprinkled with sand, designs were swept in the sand with brooms. As early as the 1720's patterns were painted freehand on floors. Two examples of this earliest floor decoration survive in Barnstable on Cape Cod. After the Revolution many floors in the 'best' rooms were stenciled in repeat patterns with running borders about a foot wide. This painted decoration substituted for expensive rugs, just as wall stenciling took the place of wallpaper. There were many color combinations for stencil designs. An unusual one is turquoise and black on a rose ground; common ones are black and white or dark red and white on yellow ochre. Stenciled floors, examples of which we show in Figs.143-6, continued in common use into the 1840's, though only a few remain in good original condition today.

Other early floor designs were similar to those used for painted floorcloths, with alternating blocks of solid or marbled color in checkerboard patterns or other geometrical designs. See the floor in the 'Strangers' Resort' inn sign (Fig. 164).

Marbleized floors, painted to resemble marble with black and white veining on gray, were contemporary with the patterned floors. This kind of floor decoration was used for many mansions and, strangely enough, was also found in some of the simple fishermen's cottages at 'Sconset on Nantucket Island.

Spatter floors, like hooked rugs, are not appropriate for colonial houses, as this form of decoration was not begun until the patterned floors went out of fashion after 1840. Spatter floors are authentic for rooms of the middle and later nineteenth-century period, and they are attractive and easily reproduced. The earlier stenciled, checkered, or marbled floor decorations can also be reproduced with little trouble, and would make fine flooring in halls or dining rooms, where the warmth of rugs is not essential. These painted or stenciled floors would also be practical in shops displaying Americana and in colonial-type restaurants and inns.

The architectural decoration we have discussed so far is characteristic chiefly of New England. The decorated barns of eastern Pennsylvania display a quite different kind of painted ornament. These barns, most plentiful in Lebanon, Berks, Montgomery, and Lehigh counties, are commonly dark red with white geometrical decorations that are often five or six feet in diameter. In Lancaster County the barns are usually yellow with white trim. One unusual barn is painted a dark olive green with white, rust, and yellow-ochre designs. Colors quite frequently used for barn patterns are yellow and blue, occasionally red and green.

The tradition of decorated barns derives from the decorated frame houses typical of Switzerland and Germany, and was originated in Pennsylvania by the prosperous farmers of Swiss and German descent who cultivated the fertile lands of eastern Pennsylvania. As they could not ornament their stone houses with painted designs, they maintained the decorative tradition by transplanting the idea from the house to the wooden face of the barn.

These farmers began to paint and decorate their fine barns about 1840, and soon after that professional painters appeared who specialized in painting barns. The route of one of these itinerant barn decorators can often be followed by the patterns he designed. One old-time painter said he used stencils for the designs, but they were more generally marked out with chalk and string, or a large wooden compass, and then painted.

The number of circular decorations on the face of the barn varied from two to seven, and even the gable ends were frequently decorated. The structural lines of the barns were usually bordered with broad white bands, which also defined the door and window trim; supplementary false arches were often painted over doors and windows. The general effect of the whole was of a huge, lively, geometrical design.

The earliest circular design was the six-lobed symbol, which was a conventionalized tulip. The star on the barns is a conventionalized pomegranate, the flower of Solomon's temple, which was symbolic of prosperity and fertility. One also sees occasional geometrically constructed heart designs, and after 1900 primitively drawn horses and cows began to be painted in the spaces formerly occupied by geometrical symbols.

These symbols are generally believed to have been intended as 'hex signs' to scare demons away—to protect the barn from lightning and the livestock from witches. It has also been said that the artificial extensions of the windows were painted so that witches trying to fly in would bump their heads and depart. The 'hex' story, picturesque as it is, has been disclaimed by the specialists in Pennsylvania barn decoration. They admit that the symbols were to some degree talismantic in origin, but believe that when they were painted on barns in the second half of the nineteenth century, they were merely intended as decoration and that even their symbolic origins had been largely forgotten. The barn decorations should probably not be considered as pictorial expressions of an old folk superstition, but simply as part of the decorative folk art of rural Pennsylvania.

These barn designs are so handsome that it is surely a good idea to restore any of the faded ones that survive on old barns and to reproduce them on new barns so that this decorative tradition does not die out. A Pennsylvanian might design his own barn decoration in the old style, and it would be interesting to use the individual designs in miniature as ornamental motifs to print or stamp on personal and household accessories, such as writing paper, bridge scorecards, matchcases, paper napkins, and paper guest towels.

How to Decorate Your House and Barn

WALLS

Planning the Design

In choosing your pattern, measure the room carefully and then select a pattern with a frieze that will fit the narrowest space between the door or window trim and the ceiling. Center the frieze on the longest wall, or over the mantelpiece, so the design unit will match at each end.

When the door or window trim goes to the ceiling, run the frieze to the trim. This means that the vertical border will end at the frieze and at the border that runs along the baseboard or chair rail.

Should stripes be desired, a plumb line hung from the ceiling, against the wall, will help guide the stencil.

It is suggested that you read Janet Waring's book, *Early American Stencils*, which is obtainable from most libraries. It reproduces about 75 examples of old wall stencils, both all-over patterns and simpler border designs.

Preparing the Walls for Decoration

Old designs for stenciled walls are frequently found on the reverse side of old wallpaper. If you are decorating an early house, remove paper carefully with water, and watch for any sign of a pattern. If any appears, make a tracing on thin tracing paper, to keep as a record or to re-use if desired.

All trace of the old paper must be removed from the wall before painting.

If the wall is already painted, wash with soap and water to remove dirt and grime.

Fill cracks in plaster with spackle or patching plaster. Sandpaper patches so that they are even with the surrounding surface.

Give wall a coat of inside wall primer purchased ready-mixed from your paint store. It may be tinted with oil color to about the color wanted for the finishing coat. Allow this to dry 24 hours.

Painting the Walls

Use any good flat wall brush 3 to 4 inches wide.

When casein paint is used, be sure brush is suitable for water-mixed paints.

Use casein or flat oil paint. Casein paint most closely approximates the old effect; flat oil paint is more practical if walls are to be washed. Using the modern flat wall paints that have been developed in recent years, you will find that one coat applied over a well-sealed wall is generally sufficient; but if you are anxious to achieve the very best results, it is recommended that you apply two coats in addition to the priming coat, allowing 24 hours to dry between each coat.

Paint a piece of already painted board and allow to dry before applying the paint to the walls. In this way you will make sure it is the color you want.

The predominating colors used for background, besides white, were yellow, gray, light blue, light green, and pink.

Materials required	Where to buy	Amount
Inside wall primer	Paint store	According to room size
Inside paint for background, flat oil or casein	Paint store	According to room size
Tube oil or casein color for tinting	Paint store	1 tube
3″ to 4″ brush	Paint store	1
Turpentine	Paint store	According to room size
Spackle or patching plaster	Paint store	1 pkg.
No. 4/0 garnet sandpaper	Paint store	Several sheets

Applying the Design

FREEHAND PATTERNS. Measure your room and make a scale drawing on paper of the walls or panels to be decorated.

Then make a drawing of your design and sketch it on the paper pattern to be sure the decoration fits the space.

After you have made any necessary corrections, chalk in the main lines on the wall. Examine from across the room to see that the design is well centered in your spaces.

Paint the design with casein paints if casein has been used for the background coat. If flat oil paint was used, paint with japan tube paints, mixed with artists' oil color to the desired shade. Thin with turpentine if necessary.

Should the oil paint seem too heavy for easy brush strokes, add a small amount of dull-finish varnish, which will not show any gloss.

Use a small design brush or quill as in other freehand work.

STENCIL DECORATION

Cutting the Stencil. Stencils may be purchased ready-cut from paint or art-supply stores, but to make a stencil from your own drawing, or from a tracing of an old design, is a simple process. The stencil as a means of decoration for wall or floor is easily used by any careful amateur.

Use either blueprint paper, extra-heavy architects' linen, or the prepared, heavy-coated stencil paper, which may be purchased at any art-supply store.

If you use blueprint paper, trace on the design, then place the paper over a piece of glass, and cut with an Exacto No. 11 or No. 16 knife. Shellac both sides of the stencil, then apply two or three coats of varnish to stiffen. Paraffin oil may be used instead of shellac. Hang on a nail to dry.

If you use the heavy architects' linen, trace the design, then cut the stencil with sharp-pointed embroidery or surgical scissors, or an Exacto knife, as described under 'Cutting the Stencil' in Chapter 1, p. 18.

The prepared stencil paper is cut with an Exacto knife.

If more than one color is being used in your design, cut a separate stencil for each color.

Leave a wide border around your stencil so as to protect your wall from brush or finger smudges.

Materials	Where to buy	Amount
Stencil paper, blueprint paper, or architects' linen	Art supply store	Size of pattern
Glass	Hardware store	Size of pattern
No. 11 or No. 16 Exacto knife	Art supply store	1
Scissors (embroidery or surgical)	Cutlery store	1 pr.
Shellac or paraffin oil	Hardware store	Small bottle
Varnish	Hardware store	Small can

Applying the Design. If the wall to be stenciled has been painted with a water-mixed casein paint, the paint for stenciling must be of the same kind. Tube casein paints are excellent.

In general the following instructions, which describe stenciling with oil paint, apply to casein paint as well, with the exception that the medium and cleaning agent are water instead of turpentine and Carbona.

Use japan paint mixed with artists' oil colors to obtain the desired shade. Squeeze the paint onto a palette or piece of window glass and mix with palette knife until the pigment is well blended. The addition of some glazing compound will stiffen the paint and reduce the danger of its creeping under the stencils.

Use turpentine as a medium and a No. 2 or No. 4 round stencil brush. Dip the brush lightly in the turpentine and then in the paint you have mixed. Stamp out some of the paint by pounding the brush on a board or piece of newspaper. Be sure that only a small amount of paint is left in the brush.

Holding the stencil firmly against the wall surface or securing it lightly with masking tape, apply the paint to the cut-out parts of the stencil. Use a circular motion and brush from the outside edges in toward the center of the opening.

Each time you move the stencil, be sure you wipe off both sides of it with a cloth dampened with Carbona.

It is a good idea to practice on paper before working on a wall. In this way you will be able to ascertain just the right amount of paint to use. If the design blurs or blots, you will know that too much paint is being used. When moving the stencil, lift it off the wall carefully so that it doesn't slide over the paint you have just applied.

Instead of using a stencil brush, you may wish to employ another method, in which a piece of upholsterers' velour is wrapped around the finger for application of color. Carbona is used as a medium in place of turpentine.

Dip the velour in the Carbona and then in the paint. Rub out excess fluid on a piece of paper and then draw the velour lightly over the stencil.

This velour-and-finger method of stenciling is preferred by some decorators because it seems to produce the same transparent effect found on old walls and floors. The colors on old walls were never shaded, so to reproduce the old effect, colors should be applied without shading.

WALL STENCILS—See Fig. 128

If the stencil design to be used calls for more than one color, several inserts may be necessary. Provision must be made for making sure that the different colored elements of the design fit into their proper places. This is done by cutting small register marks in each stencil; these marks appear in exactly the same places and enable the user to line up the pattern every time the stencil is applied.

Obviously, if more than one color is to be used, it is necessary to let one color dry thoroughly before another stencil for any other color is applied over it.

Materials	Where to buy	Amount
Background paint, flat oil or casein	Paint store	According to size of room
Japan tube and artists' colors or casein tube paints	Art supply store	1 each
Glazing compound	Paint store	Small jar
No. 2 or No. 4 stencil brush or a piece of upholsterers' velour	Art supply store Upholstery shop	1 Small piece
Turpentine	Hardware store	1 can
Glass palette	Hardware store	1
Palette knife	Art supply store	1
Carbona	Drug store	1 bottle
Piece of board		
Masking tape	Art supply store	1 roll

To Reproduce Wall Stencil Shown

1. Prepare wall for decoration according to instructions on p. 100.

2. Paint background LIGHT YELLOW, using a 3- to 4-inch wide flat brush.

3. Enlarge design according to instructions, p. 5. Cut and apply the stencil, following directions on 'Cutting the Stencil,' p. 101, and 'Applying the Design,' p. 101.

4. Beginning with frieze at center of long wall, place leaf motif in position. Hold firmly in place and apply green color as described.

Continue around the room, matching corners as well as possible and filling in with repeat units if needed.

Now do top border.

Place geometric unit in place and repeat this stencil on one entire wall before proceeding to next. Follow this procedure with each of the other large units.

When all green color is placed on the wall, allow to dry and then apply the overlay red units, and fit red leaves in the center of the frieze units.

Proceed around room, placing red units on the flower buds and in central positions as indicated, doing one wall at a time.

COLOR GUIDE

Background—LIGHT YELLOW—white tinted with chrome yellow medium and a bit of raw umber to a light, sunny tone.

Stencils (see p. 102)—Leaf centers at top and group of flower units at bottom are VERMILION—toned with a bit of raw umber. Rest of stencil units are GREEN—chrome yellow medium with Prussian blue, raw umber, and a touch of black.

In addition to materials listed under 'Enlarging the Design,' p. 5, 'Preparing the Walls for Decoration,' p. 100, 'Cutting the Stencil,' p. 101, and 'Applying the Design,' p. 101, you will need the following:

Materials	Where to buy	Amount
Flat white oil or casein wall paint	Paint store	According to size of room
Chrome yellow medium in japan	Art supply store	½ pt.
Raw umber in oil	Art supply store	1 tube
Prussian blue in oil	Art supply store	1 tube
Vermilion in japan	Art supply store	1 tube
Lamp black in oil	Art supply store	1 tube
Or casein tube paints in colors listed above	Art supply store	1 tube each
No. 2 or No. 4 stencil brushes or upholsterers' velour	Art supply store Department store	2 Small piece
3" or 4" background brush	Art supply store	1

LANDSCAPE FRESCOES. The same paints and methods are used for landscaping as for stenciling walls, described on p. 101. Rufus Porter's seven articles on *Landscape Painting on Walls of Rooms*, published in 1846 in the first volume of the *Scientific American*, give the best available description of the old technique. Anyone planning to landscape a wall will do well to read these articles. Excerpts and illustrations from them follow here.

Porter begins with instructions for mixing and applying the colors, and suggestions for laying out the design:

[103]

'Make a sky-blue by adding celestial blue to whiting . . . also make a horizon red by mixing together ten parts in bulk of whiting with two of orange red and one of chrome yellow. Then make a cloud color by mixing an indefinite small quantity of horizon red with whiting. . . The sky-blue may be applied by a large common paint brush, either new or worn; but a brush for the application of the cloud color should be large and short. . . As a general rule, a water scene—a view of the ocean or a lake—should occupy some part of the walls . . . Other parts, especially over a fire-place, will require more elevated scenes, high swells of land, with villages or prominent and elegant buildings. On the more obscure sections of the walls, especially such as are expected to be obscured by furniture, high mountains with cascades or farm-hills may be represented. Small spaces between the windows and the corners may be generally occupied by trees and shrubbery rising from the foreground, and without much regard to the distance. . .'

He goes on to tell in detail how the design should be arranged and the colors such as 'stone-brown' and 'forest green' properly applied, with different types of colors and brush strokes used for different varieties of trees. Then further practical instructions:

'In painting the pictures of steamboats, ships, and other vessels, it is convenient to have a variety of outline drawings of vessels of various kinds, sizes and positions, on paper: the back sides of these papers are to be brushed over with dry Venetian red; then by placing one of the papers against the wall, and tracing the outlines with a pointed piece of iron, bone, or wood, a copy thereof is transferred to the wall ready for coloring. The painting of houses, arbors, villages, etc., is greatly facilitated by means of stencils. . . For this purpose several stencils must be made to match each other; for example, one piece may have the form of the front of a dwelling house . . . another the form of the end of the same house . . . a third cut to represent the roof; and a fourth may be perforated for the windows. Then, by placing these successively on the wall, and painting the ground through the aperture with a large brush . . . the appearance of a house is readily produced, in a nearly finished state. . . Trees and hedge-fences . . . are formed by means of the flat bushing-brush. . . . This is dipped in the required color, and struck end-wise upon the wall, in a manner to produce . . . a cluster of small prints or spots.'

WOODWORK

Two-toned Finishes

Graining was a skill developed by early painters to make the cheaper woods and plaster resemble mahogany and other expensive woods. In the shipbuilding towns along the New England coast some of the ship painters became so skillful that an expert could hardly distinguish the graining from the natural woods. For technique, see p. 23.

Marble was also commonly imitated on woodwork in homes as well as in many of the old New England churches and meeting-houses. To marbleize woodwork the same general technique is followed as described for marbleized floors, p. 107, with the exception that flat oil paint, instead of floor enamel, is used for the undercoat. As the pattern is on an upright surface, however, care must be taken to be sure that the paint does not run; the pattern must be re-worked if it does.

Stencil Designs

The sheathing in old New England houses was occasionally stenciled with simple patterns, similar to those applied to plaster walls. These designs may be applied to painted wallboards as described for floors, p. 106.

Landscape Panels

The decorated panels, which were part of the decoration of many eighteenth-century rooms, were painted freehand with landscapes. The panel should be prepared in the same way as a wood fireboard, described below.

Fireboards

The fireboards, made of wood or canvas, covered fireplaces during the summer. They were painted freehand, most often with a scene or a still life of fruits or flowers.

PREPARING FIBEBOARD FOR DECORATION. If you are using canvas, measure the opening of your fireplace accurately and make a frame. Stretch unbleached painters' linen as tightly as possible over the frame.

Apply a sizing made with 1½ ounces of gelatin to 1 quart of water and allowed to jell. Apply to canvas and let dry thoroughly.

Smooth with sandpaper, and then apply a second coat of the sizing.

With a palette knife spread a thin layer of white lead, thinned slightly with turpentine,

over the canvas. Work well into the pores.

Allow to dry from one to three weeks, then paint on your design.

If you are using wood, sandpaper first for a smooth surface. If wood is new, apply sealing coat of clear sealer-primer or shellac thinned one-half with alcohol. Sandpaper when wood is dry.

Apply a priming coat of enamel undercoater purchased ready-mixed.

Allow to dry thoroughly, then sandpaper.

Apply a coat of flat paint tinted to background desired.

When this has dried thoroughly, it is ready for the decoration, which is painted as for any oil painting on canvas or board. It should be varnished for protection.

FLOORS

Floors, like walls, were decorated with elaborate stenciled patterns, or with freehand designs to imitate checkered tile or carpet patterns. Some were painted to look like marble. After the mid-nineteenth century they were commonly spattered in a variety of colors. The colors generally used for painted floors were gray, yellow ochre, dark green, and brown. The stenciling was most often done in black, white, yellow, green, gray, and dark red.

Directions for decorating floors follow. In every case allow the painted floor to dry 48 hours or longer. Then protect pattern with several coats of floor varnish applied 24 hours apart, remembering not to varnish on a damp or humid day. (Read section on varnishing, p. 6.) If desired, a small amount of raw umber may be added to the first two coats of varnish to soften the bright colors.

Frequent coats of varnish should be applied to the floor as it is used, or the design will soon wear off.

Freehand Patterns

Measure floor accurately and make a scale drawing on paper. Sketch in the design to see that it fits the space properly.

Give floor two coats of floor paint of the selected background color, allowing at least 24 hours to dry between each coat.

[105]

With a piece of chalk, sketch in design.

Using japan tube paint and artists' oil colors to obtain proper tint, squeeze paint from the tube onto a palette or piece of window glass. Add a little floor varnish and blend with a palette knife so that pigment is thoroughly mixed. Use large design brush and paint in the design.

Stencil Decoration

Cut stencil as described for walls, p. 101.

Prepare floor and lay out design on paper as described above.

Dip a No. 2 or No. 4 round stencil brush in turpentine. Load the brush well with the color to be applied. Stamp out most of the paint on a board or a piece of newspaper.

Hold the stencil firmly against the floor, and apply the paint to the openings in the stencil. Use a circular motion and brush from the outside edges in toward the center of the design.

When moving the stencil, lift it off the floor carefully so that it does not slide over the paint you have just applied. If the design blurs or blots, you will know that you have used too much paint, or that you have not moved the stencil properly. It is a good idea to practice on a board before working on the floor.

Each time you move the stencil, wipe both sides with a cloth dampened in Carbona or benzine, being careful not to break the ties.

Another method of applying the design is to use a piece of velour wrapped around your finger, as described for walls on p. 101.

Varnish for protection as described above.

TO STENCIL FLOOR WITH PATTERN SHOWN

1. Prepare floor for decoration as described on p. 105.

2. Measure room, marking center, and plan design so that border fits neatly at corners and is centered on hearth, if any. Plan main units to balance within border.

3. Paint background with yellow-ochre floor paint, toned with burnt umber to dull yellow-brown. Let dry 24 hours. Give floor second coat of yellow ochre. Let dry 24 hours.

4. Cut stencils as described, p. 101, after enlarging as directed, p. 5.

5. Starting with border and at center of long side, apply half-moon and leaf units, using a

No. 4 stencil brush and WHITE paint. Do one complete side before moving to another.

Apply petal units above this leaf unit in alternate colors of WHITE and BLACK, using separate stencils and brushes for each color.

When border is completely dry, begin at center of room and apply floral units in alternate BLACK and WHITE, working lengthwise down floor, and proceed to finish one side, letting any unfinished units of design end where border begins.

When this is dry, proceed to other side in same manner and allow to dry 24 hours.

6. Varnish for protection as described under 'Floors,' p. 105.

In addition to the materials listed for 'How to Prepare Wood for Decoration,' p. 5, 'To Enlarge Design,' p. 5, 'Cutting the Stencil,' p. 101, and 'Applying the Design,' p. 101, you will need:

Materials	Where to buy	Amount
Yellow-ochre floor paint	Paint store	According to size of room
Burnt umber in oil	Art supply store	1 tube
Black japan or artists' oil color	Art supply store	½ pt.
White japan or artists' oil color	Art supply store	½ pt.
4″ to 5″ brush for background	Paint store	1
4″ to 5″ varnish brush	Paint store	1
No. 4 stencil brushes	Art supply store	2
Turpentine	Paint store	½ pt.
Floor varnish	Paint store	According to size of room

FLOOR STENCILS—See Fig. 146

Marbleizing

If possible, study natural marble to learn characteristic colors, vein markings, and color shadings.

Paint the floor with two coats of flat paint, 24 hours apart, in black, white, or color to match undertone of the marble to be imitated.

Sandpaper each coat to get as smooth a ground as possible.

For a colored marble, coat the surface with a thin glaze of color, just enough to fog it. This glaze can be a glazing liquid, or a mixture of about equal parts of flat varnish, boiled linseed oil, and turpentine. To this add a little white, or any color needed for the marble you are imitating.

While this glazing color is wet, wipe out spots at irregular intervals. Using a color a few degrees darker than the ground or glazing color, put in broad veins by dipping a small paint brush in veining color and drawing through the wet glaze.

The old-time painters used a wing feather from a goose or turkey to do the veining. By dragging

[107]

it through the wet glaze some very delicate lines are made and the blending of colors is more interesting. Many modern painters still use this technique.

The simplest marble to imitate is black and white. For this the ground coat is flat black thinned with turpentine.

When this coat is dry, apply a black glaze made with ivory black and glazing liquid. On the wet glaze apply the broad veins in white with a ½ inch brush. Wipe over the white veins with a badger blender brush, or any soft, dry, flat brush. Use brush strokes light enough to soften the edges and to drag some of the black over the white. Now the fine and very fine veins are drawn in white with a very small brush.

Paint only a small area at a time, and protect your design with several coats of varnish.

Spatter

Give the floor two coats of floor enamel of the desired background color. Allow at least 24 hours to dry between each coat.

Divide one gallon of white finishing-coat paint into four quarts.

Tint each quart a different color, choosing colors that go well with each other as well as with the background color.

Use a separate brush for each color. Work on a small section of the floor at a time.

Hold a straight piece of wood in the left hand, dip the brush lightly into one of the colors, then strike the brush sharply against the straight edge, jarring droplets off the bristle ends.

Repeat with the second color, using a fresh brush and a clean piece of board.

Continue as described above with the other two colors.

Now move to another spot and repeat.

Allow to dry at least 24 hours, and then give two or three coats of floor varnish for protection.

Practice on a sample surface before applying to the floor.

PENNSYLVANIA BARN DESIGNS

The decorated circle, which is the customary 'hex sign,' is made with string and a piece of chalk used as a compass, or a large wooden compass.

The largest circle should be 4 to 6 feet across. In decorating a barn the number of circles used will be determined by the number of spaces between windows and doors. On the face of barns as few as two circles might be used, and as many as seven. When you are using only two, they should be of the same size and design, but when you use more, both the size and the design may vary.

The colors used for the symbols were most often white on a red barn; occasionally yellow, red, blue, rust, and green. The arches over windows and doors were white.

To Reproduce One of Barn Designs Shown

Since the paint will be exposed to the weather, it should be outside paint. Most of the needed colors are available in ready-mixed house paint. When special colors are desired, it will be necessary to intermix outside paint.

Lay out design with cord and chalk and fill in with paint according to chalked outlines.

Materials needed	Where to buy	Amount
Outside house paint of desired colors	Paint store	According to size of decoration
4″ brush for large units	Art supply store	1
2″ brush for smaller units	Art supply store	1
Chalk and cord	Hardware store	

PENNSYLVANIA BARN DESIGNS   [109]

114. NEW HAMPSHIRE INTERIOR IN 1824 (above)

115. JONATHAN COGSWELL HOUSE, ESSEX, MASS. (below)

116. PENNSYLVANIA DOOR

117. CONNECTICUT DOOR

118, 119. HIBBARD HOUSE, ITHACA, N.Y., AND DETAIL OF FIREBOARD

120. MASSACHUSETTS OVERMANTEL (above)   121. CONNECTICUT OVERMANTEL (below)

FALLS OF NIAGARA.

Above, below, where'er the astonished eye
Turns to behold, new opening wonders lie.

With uproar hideous, first the *Falls* appear;
The stunning tumult thundering on the ear.

There the broad river, like a lake outspread,
The islands, rapids, falls, in grandeur dread.

This great, o'erwhelming work of awful Time,
In all its dread magnificence, sublime.

122. PENNSYLVANIA FIREBOARD (above)   123. PENNSYLVANIA FIREBOARD (below)

124. FIREBOARD FROM SOUTH CAROLINA (above)   **125. CONNECTICUT FIREBOARD** (below)

126. PENNSYLVANIA FIREBOARD (above)   127. NEW ENGLAND FIREBOARD (below)

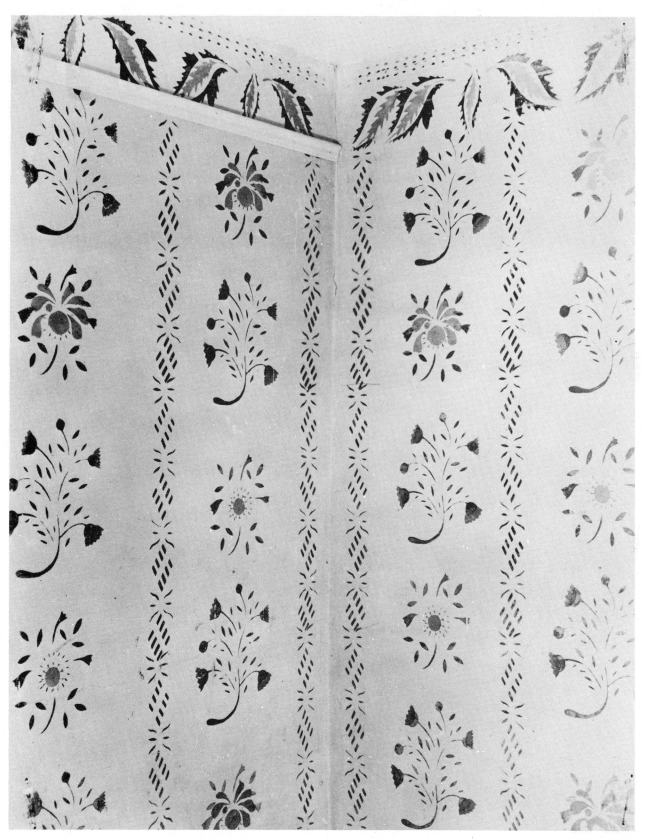

128. STENCILED WALLS IN MAINE

129. STENCILED WALLS IN NEW HAMPSHIRE

130. MAINE WALL STENCIL

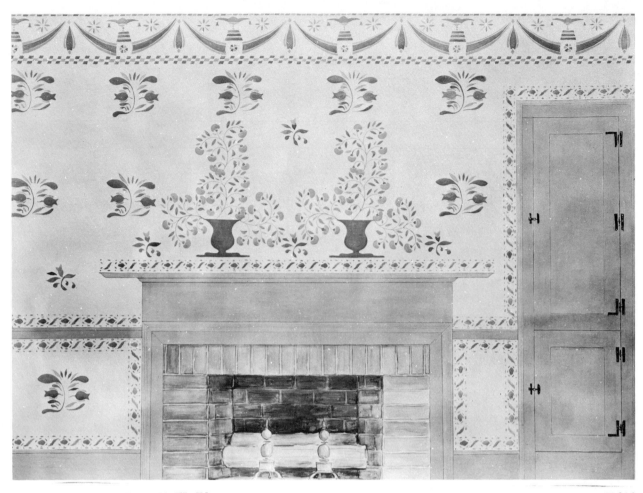

131. STENCILED OVERMANTEL IN
CONNECTICUT (above)

132. OVERMANTEL FRESCO FROM
NEW HAMPSHIRE (below)

133. OVERMANTEL FRESCO IN NEW HAMPSHIRE (above)   134. FRESCOED WALL IN MASSACHUSETTS (below)

135, 136. FRESCOED PARLOR IN MASSACHUSETTS

137. FRESCOED HALL IN MAINE

138. OVERMANTEL FRESCO IN MASSACHUSETTS

139. OVERMANTEL FRESCO IN CONNECTICUT

140, 141, 142. FRESCOED MASONIC ROOM IN NEW LEBANON, N.Y., AND DETAILS

143. STENCILED FLOOR IN MASSACHUSETTS (above)   144. STENCILED FLOOR IN CONNECTICUT (below)

145, 146. STENCILED FLOORS IN MASSACHUSETTS

147. PENNSYLVANIA BARN

148. DETAIL OF PENNSYLVANIA BARN

CHAPTER 6

COACH AND SIGN PAINTING

Ornamental Painting · Trade and Tavern Signs

Many of the famous early painters, like John Smibert, Matthew Pratt, Edward Hicks, and Chester Harding, started their careers as coach or sign painters. Chester Harding's life, as he details it in his autobiography, is a typical case history for the fine artists who started out as simple decorative painters. He was born in Conway, Massachusetts, in 1799 and began his career as a chair maker and tavern keeper. Tiring of these occupations, he migrated to Pittsburgh 'in search of adventures.' Here he opened a sign painter's shop and became acquainted with a Mr. Nelson, 'an ornamental sign and portrait painter,' as his advertisement ran. Harding became interested in portraiture and was soon a successful portrait painter, getting as fee 'the advanced price of forty dollars.' He next opened a fashionable painting room in Boston. Shortly after that he sailed to London, where he exhibited at the Royal Academy. When he returned to Boston, he was firmly established as a famous and wealthy portrait painter.

Countless painters advertised that they did 'Ornamental and Sign Painting,' 'Sign and Fancy Painting,' and 'Painting in General.' Gustavus Hesselius, who became one of the important colonial portrait painters, advertised in the *Pennsylvania Gazette* for 11 December 1840: 'Painting done in the best manner. . . Coats of Arms drawn on Coaches, Chaises, etc., or any kind of ornaments, Landskips, Sign Show Boards, Ship and House painting, Gilding of all sorts. . .'

Coach decoration was one of the chief branches of ornamental painting and served as a training school for apprentice painters. We know that a great many fine artists at one time ornamented coaches and wagons, sleighs, and fire-engine panels. This kind of craft work left its mark on the style of many of the early painters.

The Concord coaches manufactured from 1827 in Concord, New Hampshire, were among the most picturesque of the ornamented vehicles. In the 'seventies, when John Burgum, one of the best-known coach painters, was chief decorator, the Concord coach was still at its height of splendor.

Entries dated from 1858 in the Abbot-Downing Company order books for Concord coaches record just what the customers wanted in the way of decoration. Each coach was decorated to order. 'Ornament up rich and tasty' requests one entry; 'Put on some nice, neat landscape' orders another. One customer wishes something 'richly ornamental and showy' while another prefers ornament 'neat but not gaudy.' About 1865 Barney Hull, proprietor of the Sherman House in Boston, orders a nine-passenger city coach, the body to be carmine and the carriage emerald green. The name of the hotel is to be elaborately lettered, and he wishes painted 'on one door the Sherman House with all surrounding buildings, leaving off some of the vehicles. On the other door a female, or anything we please.' The ornament on the footboard is specified as 'a dancer on horseback on side of hotel and on the other side Phil Sheridan.' The Lick House in San Francisco orders for the doors 'some handsome figure' with the coat of arms of California on the footboard. The Windsor Hotel in New York specifies 'horses on one door and dogs on the other.' The Sea View House at Rye Beach, New Hampshire, wants the door to show 'a coach and horses painted in the road.'

The coaches were richly fitted out with sparkling silver-plated railings and handles, bright plush lining, and lively painted decoration. Many a time, on the arrival of one of these coaches at its destination, the whole town turned out to celebrate, brass band and all. The mail coaches and omnibuses were equally splendid with brightly painted bodies, elegant scroll work and striping, and handsome scenic paintings.

The decorated sleighs were less ornate, but some were painted with scenes much like those on the coaches. The earlier ones were painted and stenciled in the same manner as was the decorated furniture of the time. Titus Geesey described a fine example of an eighteenth-century sleigh decorated with red tulips that he saw some years ago in Pennsylvania. The early nineteenth-century cutter painted black and green (Fig. 152) is decorated with an elaborate red and yellow leaf-and-shell design.

The fire-engine panel painted by an unknown artist (Fig. 153) is typical of the kind of decoration that the old-time volunteer firemen commissioned for their cherished engines. The subject here is the coat of arms of the State of Maine; others were patriotic and mythological items, portraits of national heroes or theatrical personages or literary characters, and scenes of contemporary events. The firemen felt much the same way about the painted decoration for their engine that sailors did about their ship's figurehead, and the painting of a single engine might cost anywhere from $300 to $1000. Many notable nineteenth-century artists—including Sully, Inman, Woodside, and Quidor—at one time decorated fire engines and hose carts. John Quidor, in fact, was frequently alluded to as the 'engine artist.'

The shop and inn signs, of which large numbers of quaint examples survive, make up one of the largest groups of folk decoration. These signs are the earliest American advertising art, and the painters who decorated them were our first commercial artists. The signs were usually made with pictures on both sides to attract the attention of travelers coming from any direction. These pictorial signs, in use from the early

seventeenth century, filled a real need when many travelers could not read.

Trade signs represented whatever was for sale inside, like the array of hats and other items in Mr. Fitts' general store in Massachusetts (Fig. 166). A sign for a Providence shoe shop, dated 1718, illustrated various types of 'Butes and Shous,' which were strikingly painted in black and red on a white ground.

In Salem in 1645 it was decreed that for taverns 'there be sett up some inoffensive sign obvious for directions to strangers.' In the same year the Rhode Island courts ordered all tavern keepers to 'cause to be sett out a convenient Sign at ye most conspicuous place of ye said house, thereby to give notice to strangers it is a house of public entertainment and this to be done with all convenient speed.'

The earliest tavern signs most often represented British characters or emblems, but after the Revolution these were apt to be shot at or hacked to pieces. Eagles and portraits of Washington then led in popularity, and in the numerous signs representing the crowned royal lion the crown was painted out, leaving a realistic rather than a symbolic lion, which continued popular for signs through the mid-nineteenth century. An Englishman visiting America in 1818 wrote: 'We observed several curious tavern signs in Philadelphia and on the roadside, among others Noah's Ark; a variety of Apostles; Bunyan's Pilgrim; a cock on a lion's back crowing with Liberty issuing from his beak; naval engagements in which the British are in a desperate situation; the most common signs are eagles, heads of public characters, etc.'

Among the perennially popular tavern signs were those designed to welcome the sailors in harbor towns. At the sign of a tavern named The Anchor, visiting sailors saw a large anchor and read these lines:

> *Coil up your ropes and anchor here*
> *Till better weather doth appear.*

The Three Jolly Sailors on Water Street in Boston showed a sign with three sailors and doggerel that read:

> *Brother Sailor! please to stop*
> *And lend a hand to strap the block;*
> *For if you do not stop or call*
> *I cannot strap the block at all.*

Humorous signboards were frequently made for taverns, to stop and amuse wayfarers. One bore the picture of a headless woman and was entitled 'The Quiet Woman.' A globe with a man's head, arms, and legs was called 'Struggling Man.' Another, found in both Philadelphia and Boston, showed a tree, a bird, a ship, and a mug of beer, and four lines of verse:

> This is the tree that never grew
> This is the bird that never flew
> This is the ship that never sailed
> This is the mug that never failed.

A sign captioned 'A Man Full of Trouble' pictured a man who carried on his back a drunken woman, a monkey, and a magpie, and who wore around his neck a chain and lock marked 'Wedlock.' A popular early sign known as 'The Four Alls' showed a king, a general, a minister, and a laborer, with the legends 'I govern all,' 'I fight for all,' 'I pray for all,' and 'I pay for all.'

Mabel Swan, in an article published in the *Antiquarian,* tells an amusing anecdote about Dr. Nathaniel Ames of Dedham, Massachusetts, and the signboard he had painted in 1749 for his tavern. The sign, for which the original drawing has been preserved, was made as a jibe at two judges who failed to support Ames in a lawsuit,

and showed them with their backs turned to the book of Province Laws. The judges were eventually told of the sign and ordered a sheriff to bring it before them, but Rev. Ames heard of this. By the time the sheriff arrived, the sign had been removed and in its place hung another with the verse: 'A wicked and adulterous generation seeketh after a sign, but there shall no sign be given it.' Agile-minded Dr. Ames had signs specially designed for a unique situation, a procedure that was unusual enough to make history in eighteenth-century Dedham.

The stock subjects for the early signs were, of course, sufficiently varied to meet any ordinary needs, and the itinerant sign painters would illustrate to order Biblical, mythological, or nautical scenes; Masonic symbols, proverbs, human figures, animals, emblems, fruits, flowers, trees, and any number of other things.

Today, when so many colonial-type homes, antique shops, tea rooms, and inns hang out signs, it would be entertaining to reproduce old signboards to direct and attract the twentieth-century traveler. The fashionable type of 'shoppe' signs showing prettified, pseudo-colonial dames are dull and ordinary. It would be just as easy to copy exactly, with appropriate lettering, one of the well-designed folk signs of the early stagecoach days.

CARRIAGE STRIPING AND STENCIL DESIGNS— from *The Complete Carriage and Wagon Painter* by Fritz Schreiber, 1895. Courtesy Carl Drepperd

Methods

COACH PAINTING

The early books on carriage painting listed in the Bibliography give detailed instruction in this specialized craft, which few will wish to practice today. However, if you own an old carriage or sleigh and wish to restore it to its original condition, it will be well to consult these and other old books on coach painting. These books describe the brushes, tools, and colors needed, and methods of lettering, scrolling, ornamenting, striping, and varnishing. It is interesting to find that often in the old days a special room was used for the critical varnishing operation, and extreme care was taken to keep the room free from dust. It was made as tight as possible, wet canvas was hung around the room to settle the dust, and only the varnisher was permitted in the room.

SIGN PAINTING

To Prepare Wooden Sign for Painting

Sandpaper wood until smooth.

If there are any knotty places, scrape and coat with shellac.

Apply one coat of priming paint. Allow to dry, and then fill in any cracks or nail holes with putty. Sandpaper the surface until smooth.

The wood will need at least two coats of flat oil paint; allow 48 hours to dry between each coat.

To Decorate Sign Shown

1. Prepare the surface for painting as described above.

2. Give background two coats of BROWN flat paint, allowing 48 hours for drying between each coat.

3. Enlarge the design to fit your space and transfer to sign according to instructions in the Introduction, p. 5.

4. Letter as desired. The early *Treatise on Carriage, Sign, and Ornamental Painting*, listed in the Bibliography, gives detailed descriptions

SIGN LETTERING—from Orson Campbell's *Treatise on Carriage, Sign and Ornamental Painting*, 1841. Courtesy Carl Drepperd

and illustrations of various types of lettering of the period.

5. Paint the design, using the following colors: Background of the design—BLACK.

When background is dry, stripe the shield VERMILION and WHITE.

The eagle is GOLD, as are the shield, arrows, branch, and lettering.

To apply the gold for the eagle and the lettering, use a No. 6 lettering brush and paint with black Serviseal. Allow to become almost dry. Then rub in a quantity of bronze powder, a rich gold shade. Polish with a piece of cotton. Let dry 24 hours.

6. Varnish with three coats of spar varnish, allowing at least 24 hours to dry between each coat.

In addition to materials listed under enlarging and transferring the design, p. 5, you will need the following:

Materials required	Where to buy	Amount
Paints:		
Priming	Paint store	½ pt.
Flat brown	Paint store	½ pt.
Flat black	Paint store	½ pt.
Vermilion in japan	Paint store	1 tube
White in japan	Paint store	1 tube
Rich-gold bronze powder	Paint store	1 oz.
Black Serviseal	Paint store	Small can
Brushes:		
1" to 2" background	Paint store	2
No. 6 lettering	Paint store	1
Wood for sign	Lumber yard	According to size
2/0 sandpaper	Paint store	Several sheets
Shellac	Paint store	½ pt.
Putty	Paint store	Small can
Spar varnish	Paint store	1 pt.
Cotton	Drug store	Small piece

DETAIL OF INN SIGN—See Figs. 159 and 160

149. BROOKLYN OMNIBUS

150. CONCORD COACH

151, 152. CUTTER WITH DETAIL OF BACKBOARD

153. FIRE-ENGINE PANEL

154. PENNSYLVANIA TRADE SIGN

155. PENNSYLVANIA INN SIGN (above)

156. MASONIC INN SIGN (above)

157. CONNECTICUT TAVERN SIGN (below)

158. RHODE ISLAND TAVERN SIGN (below)

159, 160. CONNECTICUT INN SIGN

161, 162. NEW ENGLAND SHOP SIGN

163. NEW ENGLAND TRADE SIGN (above)

164. CONNECTICUT INN SIGN (below)

165. CONNECTICUT TAVERN SIGN

166. MASSACHUSETTS SHOP SIGN

CHAPTER 7

FRACTUR DESIGNS

History · Types · Artists · Sources · Style

Fractur is the quill drawing and watercolor painting that was adapted in Pennsylvania in the eighteenth and nineteenth centuries from the old European art of manuscript illumination. The art of *fraktur-schriften*, as it was called, literally means writing in Gothic type, 'fractur' being the name of a sixteenth-century German type face. This kind of decorative calligraphy, which preceded the invention of printing, was used from the eleventh century in Europe. In America it developed into a rich and decorative folk art in which the lettering was gradually subordinated to the painted decoration.

In the museum of the Bucks County Historical Society at Doylestown there is preserved a schoolmaster's fractur paint box containing the simple old materials and tools he used for his work. In it are goose-quill pens and cat's-hair brushes, small bottles containing caked colors that were once liquefied with whiskey, and cherry-gum varnish, which was occasionally used, diluted with water, to add a shining finish to the colors. The paints—blood red, golden yellow, soft blue, and delicate greens—were homemade dyes concocted from old recipes that were handed down from one generation to the next.

The art of fractur was brought to this county by the refugees from the German Palatinate, who, encouraged by William Penn, poured into the port of Philadelphia in the early eighteenth century and settled in the fertile valleys of Pennsylvania. The earliest fractur work was done in the Ephrata Cloister in Lancaster County by members of the religious community founded there in 1728 by Conrad Beissel. The art of fractur, begun in Ephrata around 1730, flourished in Pennsylvania for over two centuries, long after it had died out in Europe.

In almost every eighteenth-century group migrating to Penn's lands, a schoolmaster or minister proficient in the art of fractur writing was included in order to supply the new settlers with the needed documents for their vital statistics. For generations schoolmasters and clergymen specialized in executing these handmade certificates in order to earn a few extra dollars, though in the nineteenth century itinerant fractur artists largely monopolized the work. By 1819 the fractur vogue was so great that one Johann Krauss published an instruction book on the art as practiced in Allentown, and numerous booklets were printed to teach fractur to school children. A fractur alphabet from one of these is reprinted on p. 146. The German community schools of Pennsylvania taught illumination and Gothic lettering until the establishment of the English school system in the 'fifties. This virtually ended the period of fractur, and from about that time printed certificates took the place of the old hand-illuminated documents.

The fractur tradition, however, died hard among the custom-loving Germans, and during Civil War times people were still occasionally tracing off and using for birth and baptismal certificates designs that were fashionable in the first years of the nineteenth century. Some designs were carried over for generations with almost no change, a fact that is important to know for dating Pennsylvania fractur.

Frances Lichten, author of *Folk Art of Rural* [143]

Pennsylvania, tells about an old fractur writer named August Bauman, a veteran of the Civil War, who traveled about practicing his craft as recently as the beginning of the twentieth century. At that time he was still calling on old clients and getting new customers for baptismal and confirmation certificates by finding out from the local pastors the names of the newly baptized and recently confirmed.

The earliest fractur, begun at Ephrata, was religious in character, and continued to flourish throughout the state among the various religious sects — Mennonites, Dunkards, Schwenkfelders, Amish, and Moravians. The first fractur subjects were the prayers and hymns and book illustrations of the monastic manuscripts. Then came the ornamented documents, and a bit later schoolmasters illuminated song books and primers for school children, and made little drawings of birds or flowers as special 'rewards of merit' for diligent scholars. Bookplates and schoolbook illustrations were often drawn and colored by boys at school, and fractur certificates were occasionally made at home by members of the family. Itinerant penman specialized in family registers and certificates of birth, baptism, confirmation, marriage, and death. These were almost invariably painted in advance and lettered to order, the inscriptions being generally written in German. The fractur artists also lettered and decorated 'house blessings,' which asked for God's blessing on the family and home, moral precepts, valentines, bookplates, and bookmarks. Occasionally they made special presentation pieces like the one reproduced in Fig. 168, and some, like Fig. 170, to be framed as household decorations.

Among the best-known professional fractur artists were Francis Portzeline of Union County, who executed the piece reproduced in Fig. 174; 'Rev. Young,' who made the fractur illustrated in Fig. 169; Daniel Schumaker of Schuylkill County; and Martin Brechall, who worked in Northampton and other counties. Henrich Otto of Lancaster County was one of the great early Pennsylvania German decorators who both executed fractur and ornamented dower chests. His certificate shown in Fig. 178 is a good example of the early fracturs in which the basic lettering is printed, with the decoration painted and the

personal data lettered by hand. It is interesting to find that wedding certificates were frequently pasted inside the lids of dower chests, which were often painted for the bride by the same itinerant decorator who made her marriage certificate.

Family registers and calligraphic writing sheets of various sorts are also found in New England, New York, and other states; but these drawings are relatively few as compared with the large group of fracturs that made up an established decorative art in Pennsylvania.

Fractur is an important key to Pennsylvania folk design and a source for much of it, for many of the patterns found on furniture, utensils, and even barns were adapted from fractur designs. These designs are for the most part derived from early German folk art, with a sprinkling of New World subjects such as American eagles and portraits of our national heroes. In order to grasp the full significance of Pennsylvania fractur, as well as its purely aesthetic character as a folk art, it is important to understand that some symbolism lay behind most of the popular motifs. The tulip, for instance, was cherished as an important item of commerce in Europe and also had a religious meaning, the three petals symbolizing the Trinity and commonly accepted in Germany as a variation of the Holy Lily. Mermaids symbolized the dual nature of Christ—half man, half deity. Lions, crowns, and unicorns were popular old heraldic symbols, and as on dower chests the unicorns on fractur certificates represented virginity, and hearts represented love and marriage. A clock painted on one birth certificate indicated the exact time the child was born. Almost every element in a fractur had some specific connotation, so that the painted design as well as the inscriptions were meaningful to the owner.

Some of the common fractur motifs, like the pomegranates that are traditional in Persian textile patterns, are strongly reminiscent of Persian and Indo-Persian art, which at first glance seems a puzzling source for these designs. But Persian damasks were being reproduced by German block printing as early as the twelfth century, and by the fifteenth century the influence of Persian painting and fabrics was very strong in Germany. This influence was carried across the seas and found expression in some of the fractur pieces of the Pennsylvania Germans, in which German, Asiatic, and American motifs blend to form a rich, cosmopolitan folk art.

Fractur motifs were almost entirely derivative, but it is interesting to observe that fractur developed its own style on American soil—a more primitive kind of design and more robust coloring than was typical of similar work abroad. The evolution of this American fractur style can be traced from the early eighteenth century, when it was close to German illuminated manuscripts, through the first half of the nineteenth century, when, like other American art forms, it became relatively independent of its forbears. In the earliest fractur the letters and ornamental designs are finely drawn and elaborately detailed, the colors soft and subtle. The painting is subordinated to the inscriptions in the early work, as it was in the old illuminated manuscripts. In the later pieces the drawing and lettering are cruder, the painted designs bolder, and the colors much stronger and brighter.

It is generally thought that the older the fractur, the more desirable it is as early Americana. This critical opinion should be revised, for it was not until the Pennsylvania German artists adapted themselves to the new pioneer environment in America that they developed a fresh, free approach. It is this new native style that makes the later eighteenth- and early nineteenth-century fracturs much more interesting as American folk art than the earliest ones, which were so completely a part of the established European tradition. It will be found that the outstanding fractur masterpieces, from the point of view of original design, date from the late 1700's and early 1800's rather than from the pre-Revolutionary period. This is equally true of all the other branches of early American art, for America achieved artistic as well as political independence after the Revolution.

Pennsylvania fractur is one of the most interesting products of our rural-art tradition, and the quality of design in the best examples is unsurpassed in the field of decorative watercolors. The piece in the Karolik collection (Fig. 168) has the strong, staccato rhythm of a folk dance, which is pictorially carried out in the scissors-like gestures of the facing couple, the

thrusting, stylized branches of the plant, and even in the details of dress, in which repeated small triangles echo the larger angular shapes in an animated point and counterpoint of design. The presentation piece drawn for one Elizabeth Fedderly in 1818 and the formalized portrayal of 'exselenc georg' and 'Ledy Waschingdon' (Figs. 170 and 181) are fine examples of Pennsylvania watercolor decoration at its peak. The boldly drawn and colored Bingeman baptismal certificate (Fig. 177) is unique in its suggestion of the design of a stained-glass window. Its balanced pattern contrasts with the haphazard and naïve but somehow charming Sarah Campion birth certificate (Fig. 179), in which the large lettered caption was so casually executed that there was no room at the margin for the final N of the name.

Fractur designs are infinitely varied in content and style, and in their time they served a great many purposes. Most of the fracturs were so simply drawn and colored that they are easy to reproduce, and the different kinds may be used in a variety of ways. If you live in Pennsylvania, you should certainly consider making valentines or a bookplate like some of the early fractur examples, making a birth certificate for your child, or designing your Christmas card from an appropriate fractur detail such as the primitive angel at the top of Fig. 180. Any of the typical fractur motifs would make an attractive bit of design for some special writing paper. A personal family register could be made by lettering the vital statistics for your family in the framework of a fractur such as the ones we reproduce in Figs. 169 and 176.

Fractur has become an immensely popular item for collectors, and single examples are featured as decorative pieces in homes throughout the country. Any of the fracturs illustrated might well be reproduced in ink and watercolor. The interesting two-toned Pennsylvania frame shown in Fig. 67 originally contained a fractur and so would be an authentic one to duplicate for your fractur reproduction. An accurate watercolor copy of one of the masterpiece fracturs, appropriately framed, would make an outstanding decoration for any room furnished in the early American manner.

Technique for Reproduction

Enlarge the design to the desired size according to instructions on p. 5. The early fracturs ranged from about 14 by 18 inches for large certificates, down to a few inches for bookmarks and 'rewards of merit.'

Lay a piece of transparent tracing paper over the design and trace carefully.

Go over the lines on the reverse side of the tracing paper with a soft pencil. Retrace onto paper to be used for fractur.

With India ink, sepia and black mixed to get old brownish-black color, and with a crow-quill pen, go over the outlines, being careful to keep the lines smooth and even.

Paint the design with watercolors, using a No. 3 or No. 4 brush for fine work and No. 5 for

OLD FRACTUR ALPHABET—from *Deutsch & Englische Vorschriften fur die Jugend* by Carl Friederich Egelmann, *c.*1846. Courtesy Carl Drepperd

BIRTH AND BAPTISMAL CERTIFICATE—See Fig. 169

larger spaces. Liquid transparent watercolors are now available at many art supply stores. You may find it easier to obtain even distribution of color with them than with pan or tube colors. The colors in some old fracturs have a slight gloss. To reproduce this effect mix colors with beaten egg (white and yolk), or varnish colored areas with diluted varnish.

For the script write the German letters in ink, sepia and black mixed, using the same type of letters as on the original manuscript if possible.

Use any ivory or cream-color paper that will take ink and watercolor. Old paper—the flyleaves of old books, or the blank pages of old ledgers or drawing books—will make the most authentic-looking reproduction.

TO REPRODUCE FRACTUR SHOWN

Follow instructions above for applying design and lettering, and use the following colors:

The two urns are BLUE with a RED knob.

The petal decoration at top and base of urn is a black-ink outline over the blue, with the center petal YELLOW.

The band around the middle of the urn is YELLOW with a RED line.

The band at the stem and around the bottom is RED.

The shelf is RED, BLUE, YELLOW, BLUE, RED, YELLOW, BLUE, BLUE, RED. The next band is WHITE with YELLOW scrolls at each end. Next comes RED, YELLOW with RED lines, BLUE, RED, BLUE.

The tops of the pilasters are YELLOW with BLACK tracing, RED, YELLOW, RED.

A black pen-and-ink line divides each color. Pilasters are BLUE with black lines.

The left-hand figure has a WHITE dress with RED and GREEN flowers. (Center petal RED, outer petals GREEN.)

The right-hand figure has a YELLOW dress.

Each dress has a BLUE band around the sleeve and a BLUE sash.

The mantle over the shoulder is RED with black lines.

The skin is FLESH COLOR with PINK cheeks, BLACK hair and features.

The scrolls held in the hands are WHITE with black script.

The melon-shaped object held by the left-hand figure is WHITE with black script, a YELLOW band, and BLACK handle.

The anchor held by the right-hand figure is BLACK.

Shoes are WHITE.

Top band across bottom of picture, YELLOW. Small sections at each side, BLUE. Same section at center, WHITE. Bottom band, RED.

COLOR GUIDE

YELLOW—mustard yellow—brown added to clear yellow.

BLUE—deep sky-blue.

RED—brick red—brown added to red.

GREEN—light leaf shade.

PINK—red and white.

FLESH—white, yellow, and red.

WHITE—unpainted.

BLACK—mixture of black and sepia India ink.

In addition to materials listed under 'To Enlarge Design,' p. 5, you will need the following:

Materials	Where to buy	Amount
Watercolors:		
Yellow	Art supply store	Smallest quantity
Blue	Art supply store	Smallest quantity
Black	Art supply store	Smallest quantity
Red	Art supply store	Smallest quantity
Green	Art supply store	Smallest quantity
Brown	Art supply store	Smallest quantity
White	Art supply store	Smallest quantity
Watercolor brushes:		
No. 3 or No. 4	Art supply store	1
No. 5	Art supply store	1
Crow-quill pen	Art supply store	1
India ink, black and sepia	Art supply store	1 bottle of each
Tracing paper	Art supply store	1 sheet
No. 3 hard pencil	Art supply store	1
Soft pencil	Art supply store	1
Ivory-color paper for the picture	Art supply store	1 sheet

167. BIRTH CERTIFICATE (above)   168. PRESENTATION PIECE (below)

169. BIRTH AND BAPTISMAL CERTIFICATE

170. PORTRAIT OF GEORGE AND MARTHA WASHINGTON

172. VALENTINE

171. BOOKPLATE

173. MUSIC BOOK

174. BIRTH CERTIFICATE (above)

175. BIRTH CERTIFICATE (above)

176. FAMILY REGISTER (below)

177. BIRTH AND BAPTISMAL CERTIFICATE (below)

178. BIRTH CERTIFICATE (above)

179. BIRTH CERTIFICATE (below)

[154]

180. BIRTH AND BAPTISMAL CERTIFICATE (above)   181. PRESENTATION PIECE (below)

Bibliography

GENERAL

Anonymous, *Painting and Decorating Craftsman's Manual and Text Book*, T. Audel & Co., N.Y., 1949
Bench & Brush Publications, Cohasset, Mass.
Brazer, E. S., *Early American Decoration*, Pond-Ekberg, Springfield, Mass., 1940.
Christensen, E. O., *The Index of American Design*, Macmillan, N.Y., 1950.
The Decorator, Journal of the Esther Stevens Brazer Guild of the Historical Society of Early American Decoration, Inc.
Dow, G. F., *The Arts and Crafts in New England 1704-1775*, Wayside Press, Topsfield, Mass., 1927
Drepperd, C. W., *The Primer of American Antiques*, Doubleday, N.Y., 1945.
Dutch Boy Painter Magazine, National Lead Co., N.Y.
Fraser, E. S., 'Painted Decoration in Colonial Homes,' *Cambridge Historical Society Proceedings*, Cambridge, Mass., 1936, 50-57.
Gould, M. E., *Early American Wooden Ware*, Pond-Ekberg, Springfield, Mass., 1942, Chapter 1, 'The Beginning of Paint.'
Keyser, C. N., *Pennsylvania German Design* (Home Craft Course), Mrs. C. Naaman Keyser, Plymouth Meeting, Pa., 1943.
Knust, William, *Handbook on Painting*, National Lead Co., N.Y., 1926.
Lichten, Frances, *Folk Art of Rural Pennsylvania*, Scribner's, N. Y., 1946.
Porter, Rufus, 'The Art of Painting—Ornamental Painting,' *Scientific American*, 25 December 1845.
Robacker, E. F., *Pennsylvania Dutch Stuff*, University of Pennsylvania Press, Philadelphia, 1944.
Taubes, Frederick, *Studio Secrets*, Watson-Guptill, N.Y., 1943.
Vanderwalker, F. N., *Drake's Cyclopedia of Painting and Decorating*, F. J. Drake & Co., Chicago, 1945.
Whitmore, E. M., 'Origins of Pennsylvania Folk Art,' *Antiques*, September 1940, 106-10.
Wright, Richardson, *Hawkers and Walkers in Early America*, Lippincott, Philadelphia, 1927.

FURNITURE

Dundore, R. H., *Pennsylvania German Painted Furniture* (Home Craft Course), Mrs. C. Naaman Keyser, Plymouth Meeting, Pa., 1946.
Fraser, E. S., 'The Golden Age of Stenciling,' *Antiques*, April 1922, 162-6.
'Painted Furniture in America. 1. The Period of Stenciling,' *Antiques*, September 1924, 141-6.
'Pennsylvania Bride Boxes and Dower Chests—Country Types of Chests,' *Antiques*, August 1925, 79-84.
'Pennsylvania German Dower Chests Signed by the Decorators,' *Antiques*, February 1927, 119-23; April 1927, 208-83; June 1927, 474-6.
'Pioneer Furniture from Hampton, New Hampshire,' *Antiques*, April 1930, 312-16.
'The Tantalizing Chests of Taunton,' *Antiques*, April 1933, 135-8.

Lichten, Frances, *Pennsylvania German Chests* (Home Craft Course), Mrs. C. Naaman Keyser, Plymouth Meeting, Pa., n.d.

Loncope, Henry, 'Some Rescued Stencils of Earlier Days,' *Antiques*, April 1922, 159-61.

Robinson, O. C., 'Signed Stenciled Chairs of W. P. Eaton,' *Antiques*, August 1949, 112-13.

Roy, L. M. A., 'Redecorating a Hitchcock Chair,' *Antiques*, August 1949, 110-12.

ACCESSORIES

Fraser, E. S., 'Pennsylvania Bride Boxes and Dower Chests,' *Antiques*, July 1925, 20-23.

Hoke, E. S., *Pennsylvania German Reverse Painting on Glass* (Home Craft Course), Mrs. C. Naaman Keyser, Plymouth Meeting, Pa., 1946.

Porter, Rufus, 'The Art of Painting—Painting on Glass,' *Scientific American*, 20 November 1845.

TIN

Blanchard, R. R., *How to Paint Trays*, C. T. Branford Co., Boston, 1949.

Brazer, E. S., 'Buller Tinware from Brandy Hill, Greenville, New York,' *Antiques*, August 1945, 84-7.
'The Tinsmiths of Stevens Plains,' *Antiques*, Part I, June 1939, 294-6; Part II, September 1939, 134-6.

Fraser, E. S., 'Zachariah Brackett Stevens,' *Antiques*, March 1936, 98-102.

Hoke, E. S., *Pennsylvania German Painted Tin* (Home Craft Course), Mrs. C. Naaman Keyser, Plymouth Meeting, Pa., 1946.

Robacker, E. F., 'The Case for Pennsylvania German Tin,' *Antiques*, October 1947, 263-5.

Swan, M. M., 'The Village Tinsmith,' *Antiques*, March 1928, 211-14.

Woodman, A. C., *Decorating Country Tin*, The Country Loft, Hingham, Mass., 1947.

FABRICS

Dreppard, C. W., 'Early American Painted Floor Cloths,' *Town and Country*, December 1943, 136-7, 148.

Howe, F. T., 'Three Stenciled Counterpanes,' *Antiques*, March 1940, 120-22.

King, E. W., 'Painted Window Shades,' *Antiques*, December 1939, 288-91.

Porter, Rufus, *A Select Collection of Valuable and Curious Arts and Interesting Experiments*, S. B. Moore, Concord, N.Y., 1825 (Painting on Carpets and Window Shades).

Winchester, Alice, 'Stenciled Coverlets,' *Antiques*, September 1945, 145.

ARCHITECTURE

Brazer, E. S., 'Murals in Upper New York State,' *Antiques*, September 1945, 148-9.
'Signed and Dated—A Painted Wall in Connecticut,' *Antiques*, September 1945, 138.

Karr, Louise, 'Old Westwood Murals,' *Antiques*, April 1926, 231-6.

Lipman, Jean, *American Primitive Painting*, Oxford, N. Y., 1942; Dover reprint, 1972 (Wall Decorations).

Little, N. F., 'Winthrop Chandler,' *Art in America*, April 1947.

Porter, Rufus, 'Landscape Painting on Walls of Rooms,' seven articles in *Scientific American*, vol. 1, 5 February—9 April, 1846.

Selden, M. W., 'Colors Used in Early Wall Painting,' *Antiques*, May 1949, 354.

Stoudt, J. J., 'The Decorated Barns of Eastern Pennsylvania' (Home Craft Course), Mrs. C. Naaman Keyser, Plymouth Meeting, Pa., 1945.

Waring, Janet, *Early American Stencils on Walls and Furniture*, Scott, N. Y., 1937; Dover reprint, 1968.

[158] Yates, Elizabeth, 'We Found Patterns on our Walls,' *American Home*, October 1943, 30-34.

COACH AND SIGN PAINTING

Burgum, E. G., 'The Concord Coach,' *Colorado Magazine*, September 1939, 173-80.

Campbell, Orson, *Treatise on Carriage, Sign, and Ornamental Painting*, James Bailey's Press, De Ruyter, N.Y., 1841.

Chapin, H. M., *Early American Signboards, Rhode Island Historical Society*, Providence, 1926.

Dunlap, William, *A History of the Rise and Progress of the Arts of Design in the United States*, 1834. Dover reprint, 1969. (Chester Harding's biography, v. 2, 289-295.)

Hunt, E. M., 'Abbot-Downing and the Concord Coach,' *Historical New Hampshire*, New Hampshire Historical Society, November 1945, 1-20.

Schreiber, Fritz, *The Complete Carriage and Wagon Painter*, M. T. Richardson Co., N.Y., 1895.

Smith, J. J., 'Painted Fire Engine Panels,' *Antiques*, November 1937, 245-7.

Swan, M. M., Early Sign Painters,' *Antiques*, May 1928, 402-5.

'Quaint and Creaking Tavern Signs,' *Antiquarian*, May 1927, 27-30.

Porter, Rufus, 'The Art of Painting—Carriage Painting,' *Scientific American*, 9 October 1845.

'The Art of Painting—Sign Painting,' *Scientific American*, 16 October 1845.

FRACTUR

(Cahill, Holger), Museum of Modern Art Catalogue, *American Folk Art*, N.Y., 1932.

Downs, Joseph, *Pennsylvania German Arts and Crafts*, Metropolitan Museum of Art, N.Y., 1949.

Egelmann, C. F., *Deutsche & Englische Vorschriften fur die Jugend*, Reading, Pa., c.1846.

Ford, Alice, *Pictorial Folk Art New England to California*, Studio Publications, N.Y., 1949.

(Halpert, E. G.), Colonial Williamsburg Catalogue, *American Folk Art*, Williamsburg, Va., 1940.

Mercer, H. C., *The Survival of the Medieval Art of Illuminative Writing Among Pennsylvania Germans*, Bucks County Historical Society, 1897.

Shelley, D. A., 'Illuminated Birth Certificates,' *New York Historical Society Bulletin*, April 1945, 92-105. 1945, 92-105.

Selected Public Collections of Early Decoration

CONNECTICUT
Wadsworth Atheneum, Brainard Collection, Hartford—Signs.

DELAWARE
Henry Francis du Pont Winterthur Museum, Wilmington (by permission)—All types of decorated pieces.

ILLINOIS
Art institute of Chicago—Furniture, fractur.

MASSACHUSETTS
Old Deerfield—Painted and stenciled walls in a number of houses; decorated objects in Memorial Hall.
Old Sturbridge Village—Furniture, accessories, tinware, signs.
Society for the Preservation of New England Antiquities, Harrison Gray Otis House, Boston—Furniture, tinware, and Waring Collection of wall and furniture stencils.

MICHIGAN
Edison Institute Museum, Dearborn—Coaches and sleighs.

NEW HAMPSHIRE
Goyette Museum of Americana, Peterboro—Room of wall frescoes.

NEW YORK
Metropolitan Museum of Art, New York City—All types of decorated pieces in the American Wing; large collection of furniture stencils in the Print Department.
New York Historical Society, New York City—Pennsylvania collection.
New York State Historical Association, Fennimore House, Cooperstown—Group of fireboards and examples of other decorated pieces.

PENNSYLVANIA
Bucks County Historical Society, Doylestown—Pennsylvania collection, including fractur painter's kit.
Philadelphia Museum of Art—Pennsylvania collection.

VERMONT
Shelburne Museum—Furniture and accessories.

VIRGINIA
Mrs. John D. Rockefeller, Jr. Collection of Folk Art, Ludwell Paradise House, Colonial Williamsburg—Fractur group.

WASHINGTON, D.C.
National Gallery of Art, Index of American Design—About 300 watercolor renderings of decorated material of all types.
U. S. National Museum, Greenwood Collection—Various examples of decorated pieces and set of furniture stencils.

Index

[162]

Dover Books on Art

Dover Books on Art

MASTERPIECES OF FURNITURE, Verna Cook Salomonsky. Photographs and measured drawings of some of the finest examples of Colonial American, 17th century English, Windsor, Sheraton, Hepplewhite, Chippendale, Louis XIV, Queen Anne, and various other furniture styles. The textual matter includes information on traditions, characteristics, background, etc. of various pieces. 101 plates. Bibliography. 224pp. 7⅞ x 10¾.

21381-1 Paperbound $4.50

PRIMITIVE ART, Franz Boas. In this exhaustive volume, a great American anthropologist analyzes all the fundamental traits of primitive art, covering the formal element in art, representative art, symbolism, style, literature, music, and the dance. Illustrations of Indian embroidery, paleolithic paintings, woven blankets, wing and tail designs, totem poles, cutlery, earthenware, baskets and many other primitive objects and motifs. Over 900 illustrations. 376pp. 5⅜ x 8.   20025-6 Paperbound $3.75

AN INTRODUCTION TO A HISTORY OF WOODCUT, A. M. Hind. Nearly all of this authoritative 2-volume set is devoted to the 15th century—the period during which the woodcut came of age as an important art form. It is the most complete compendium of information on this period, the artists who contributed to it, and their technical and artistic accomplishments. Profusely illustrated with cuts by 15th century masters, and later works for comparative purposes. 484 illustrations. 5 indexes. Total of xi+838pp. 5⅜ x 8½. Two-vols. 20952-0,20953-0 Paperbound $10.50

A HISTORY OF ENGRAVING AND ETCHING, A. M. Hind. Beginning with the anonymous masters of .15th century engraving, this highly regarded and thorough survey carries you through Italy, Holland, and Germany to the great engravers and beginnings of etching in the 16th century, through the portrait engravers, master etchers, practicioners of mezzotint, crayon manner and stipple, aquatint, color prints, to modern etching in the period just prior to World War I. Beautifully illustrated —sharp clear prints on heavy opaque paper. Author's preface. 3 appendixes. 111 illustrations. xviii + 487 pp. 5⅜ x 8½.

20954-7 Paperbound $5.00

ART STUDENTS' ANATOMY, E. J. Farris. Teaching anatomy by using chiefly living objects for illustration, this study has enjoyed long popularity and success in art courses and home-study programs. All the basic elements of the human anatomy are illustrated in minute detail, diagrammed and pictured as they pass through common movements and actions. 158 drawings, photographs, and roentgenograms. Glossary of anatomical terms. x + 159pp. 5⅝ x 8⅜.   20744-7 Paperbound $2.50

COLONIAL LIGHTING, A. H. Hayward. The only book to cover the fascinating story of lamps and other lighting devices in America. Beginning with rush light holders used by the early settlers, it ranges through the elaborate chandeliers of the Federal period, illustrating 647 lamps. Of great value to antique collectors, designers, and historians of arts and crafts. Revised and enlarged by James R. Marsh. xxxi + 198pp. 5⅝ x 8¼.

20975-X Paperbound $3.50

Dover Books on Art

PINE FURNITURE OF EARLY NEW ENGLAND, R. H. Kettell. Over 400 illustrations, over 50 working drawings of early New England chairs, benches, beds, cupboards, mirrors, shelves, tables, other furniture esteemed for simple beauty and character. "Rich store of illustrations . . . emphasizes the individuality and varied design," ANTIQUES. 413 illustrations, 55 working drawings. 475pp. 8 x 10¾.   20145-7   Clothbound $12.50

BASIC BOOKBINDING, A. W. Lewis. Enables both beginners and experts to rebind old books or bind paperbacks in hard covers. Treats materials, tools; gives step-by-step instruction in how to collate a book, sew it, back it, make boards, etc. 261 illus. Appendices. 155pp. 5⅜ x 8.   20169-4   Paperbound $1.75

DESIGN MOTIFS OF ANCIENT MEXICO, J. Enciso. Nearly 90% of these 766 superb designs from Aztec, Olmec, Totonac, Maya, and Toltec origins are unobtainable elsewhere. Contains plumed serpents, wind gods, animals, demons, dancers, monsters, etc. Excellent applied design source. Originally $17.50. 766 illustrations, thousands of motifs. 192pp. 6⅛ x 9¼.
                    20084-1   Paperbound $2.50

A DIDEROT PICTORIAL ENCYCLOPEDIA OF TRADES AND INDUSTRY. Manufacturing and the Technical Arts in Plates Selected from "L'Encyclopédie ou Dictionnaire Raisonné des Sciences, des Arts, et des Métiers," of Denis Diderot, edited with text by C. Gillispie. Over 2000 illustrations on 485 full-page plates. Magnificent 18th-century engravings of men, women, and children working at such trades as milling flour, cheesemaking, charcoal burning, mining, silverplating, shoeing horses, making fine glass, printing, hundreds more, showing details of machinery, different steps in sequence, etc. A remarkable art work, but also the largest collection of working figures in print, copyright-free, for art directors, designers, etc. Two vols. 920pp. 9 x 12. Heavy library cloth.   22284-5, 22283-3   Two volume set $30.00

SILK SCREEN TECHNIQUES, J. Biegeleisen, M. Cohn. A practical step-by-step home course in one of the most versatile, least expensive graphic arts processes. How to build an inexpensive silk screen, prepare stencils, print, achieve special textures, use color, etc. Every step explained, diagrammed. 149 illustrations, 201pp. 6⅛ x 9¼.   20433-2   Paperbound $2.50

STICKS AND STONES, Lewis Mumford. An examination of forces influencing American architecture: the medieval tradition in early New England, the classical influence in Jefferson's time, the Brown Decades, the imperial facade, the machine age, etc. "A truly remarkable book," SAT. REV. OF LITERATURE. 2nd revised edition. 21 illus. xvii + 240pp. 5⅜ x 8.
                    20202-X   Paperbound $2.50

THE AUTOBIOGRAPHY OF AN IDEA, Louis Sullivan. The architect whom Frank Lloyd Wright called "the master," records the development of the theories that revolutionized America's skyline. 34 full-page plates of Sullivan's finest work. New introduction by R. M. Line. xiv + 335pp. 5⅜ x 8.
                    20281-X   Paperbound $3.50

200 DECORATIVE TITLE-PAGES, edited by A. Nesbitt. Fascinating and informative from a historical point of view, this beautiful collection of decorated titles will be a great inspiration to students of design, commercial artists, advertising designers, etc. A complete survey of the genre from the first known decorated title to work in the first decades of this century. Bibliography and sources of the plates. 222pp. 8⅜ x 11¼.

21264-5 Paperbound $5.00

ON THE LAWS OF JAPANESE PAINTING, H. P. Bowie. This classic work on the philosophy and technique of Japanese art is based on the author's first-hand experiences studying art in Japan. Every aspect of Japanese painting is described: the use of the brush and other materials; laws governing conception and execution; subjects for Japanese paintings, etc. The best possible substitute for a series of lessons from a great Oriental master. Index. xv + 117pp. + 66 plates. 6⅛ x 9¼.

20030-2 Paperbound $4.50

A HANDBOOK-OF ANATOMY FOR ART STUDENTS, Arthur Thomson. This long-popular text teaches any student, regardless of level of technical competence, all the subtleties of human anatomy. Clear photographs, numerous line sketches and diagrams of bones, joints, etc. Use it as a text for home study, as a supplement to life class work, or as a lifelong sourcebook and reference volume. Author's prefaces. 67 plates, containing 40 line drawings, 86 photographs—mostly full page. 211 figures. Appendix. Index. xx + 459pp. 5⅜ x 8⅜. 21163-0 Paperbound $5.00

WHITTLING AND WOODCARVING, E. J. Tangerman. With this book, a beginner who is moderately handy can whittle or carve scores of useful objects, toys for children, gifts, or simply pass hours creatively and enjoyably. "Easy as well as instructive reading," N. Y. Herald Tribune Books. 464 illustrations, with appendix and index. x + 293pp. 5½ x 8⅛.

20965-2 Paperbound $2.75

ONE HUNDRED AND ONE PATCHWORK PATTERNS, Ruby Short McKim. Whether you have made a hundred quilts or none at all, you will find this the single most useful book on quiltmaking. There are 101 full patterns (all exact size) with full instructions for cutting and sewing. In addition there is some really choice folklore about the origin of the ingenious pattern names: "Monkey Wrench," "Road to California," "Drunkard's Path," "Crossed Canoes," to name a few. Over 500 illustrations. 124 pp. 7⅞ x 10¾. 20773-0 Paperbound $2.50

ART AND GEOMETRY, W. M. Ivins, Jr. Challenges the idea that the foundations of modern thought were laid in ancient Greece. Pitting Greek tactile-muscular intuitions of space against modern visual intuitions, the author, for 30 years curator of prints, Metropolitan Museum of Art, analyzes the differences between ancient and Renaissance painting and sculpture and tells of the first fruitful investigations of perspective. x + 113pp. 5⅜ x 8⅜. 20941-5 Paperbound $2.00

PRINCIPLES OF ART HISTORY, H. Wölfflin. This remarkably instructive work demonstrates the tremendous change in artistic conception from the 14th to the 18th centuries, by analyzing 164 works by Botticelli, Dürer, Hobbema, Holbein, Hals, Titian, Rembrandt, Vermeer, etc., and pointing out exactly what is meant by "baroque," "classic," "primitive," "picturesque," and other basic terms of art history and criticism. "A remarkable lesson in the art of seeing," SAT. REV. OF LITERATURE. Translated from the 7th German edition. 150 illus. 254pp. 6⅛ x 9¼.   20276-3 Paperbound $3.50

FOUNDATIONS OF MODERN ART, A. Ozenfant. Stimulating discussion of human creativity from paleolithic cave painting to modern painting, architecture, decorative arts. Fully illustrated with works of Gris, Lipchitz, Léger, Picasso, primitive, modern artifacts, architecture, industrial art, much more. 226 illustrations. 368pp. 6⅛ x 9¼.   20215-1 Paperbound $5.00

METALWORK AND ENAMELLING, H. Maryon. Probably the best book ever written on the subject. Tells everything necessary for the home manufacture of jewelry, rings, ear pendants, bowls, etc. Covers materials, tools, soldering, filigree, setting stones, raising patterns, repoussé work, damascening, niello, cloisonné, polishing, assaying, casting, and dozens of other techniques. The best substitute for apprenticeship to a master metalworker. 363 photos and figures. 374pp. 5½ x 8½.
22702-2 Paperbound $3.50

SHAKER FURNITURE, E. D. and F. Andrews. The most illuminating study of Shaker furniture ever written. Covers chronology, craftsmanship, houses, shops, etc. Includes over 200 photographs of chairs, tables, clocks, beds, benches, etc. "Mr. & Mrs. Andrews know all there is to know about Shaker furniture," Mark Van Doren, NATION. 48 full-page plates. 192pp. 7⅞ x 10¾.   20679-3 Paperbound $4.00

LETTERING AND ALPHABETS, J. A. Cavanagh. An unabridged reissue of "Lettering," containing the full discussion, analysis, illustration of 89 basic hand lettering styles based on Caslon, Bodoni, Gothic, many other types. Hundreds of technical hints on construction, strokes, pens, brushes, etc. 89 alphabets, 72 lettered specimens, which may be reproduced permission-free. 121pp. 9¾ x 8.   20053-1 Paperbound $2.50

THE HUMAN FIGURE IN MOTION, Eadweard Muybridge. The largest collection in print of Muybridge's famous high-speed action photos. 4789 photographs in more than 500 action-strip-sequences (at shutter speeds up to 1/6000th of a second) illustrate men, women, children—mostly undraped—performing such actions as walking, running, getting up, lying down, carrying objects, throwing, etc. "An unparalleled dictionary of action for all artists," AMERICAN ARTIST. 390 full-page plates, with 4789 photographs. Heavy glossy stock, reinforced binding with headbands. 7⅞ x 10¾.   20204-6 Clothbound $12.50

ART ANATOMY, Dr. William Rimmer. One of the few books on art anatomy that are themselves works of art, this is a faithful reproduction (rearranged for handy use) of the extremely rare masterpiece of the famous 19th century anatomist, sculptor, and art teacher. Beautiful, clear line drawings show every part of the body—bony structure, muscles, features, etc. Unusual are the sections on falling bodies, foreshortenings, muscles in tension, grotesque personalities, and Rimmer's remarkable interpretation of emotions and personalities as expressed by facial features. It will supplement every other book on art anatomy you are likely to have. Reproduced clearer than the lithographic original (which sells for $500 on up on the rare book market.) Over 1,200 illustrations. xiii + 153pp. 7¾ x 10¾.

20908-3 Paperbound $3.75

THE CRAFTSMAN'S HANDBOOK, Cennino Cennini. The finest English translation of IL LIBRO DELL' ARTE, the 15th century introduction to art technique that is both a mirror of Quatrocento life and a source of many useful but nearly forgotten facets of the painter's art. 4 illustrations. xxvii + 142pp. D. V. Thompson, translator. 5⅜ x 8. 20054-X Paperbound $2.50

THE BROWN DECADES, Lewis Mumford. A picture of the "buried renaissance" of the post-Civil War period, and the founding of modern architecture (Sullivan, Richardson, Root, Roebling), landscape development (Marsh, Olmstead, Eliot), and the graphic arts (Homer, Eakins, Ryder). 2nd revised, enlarged edition. Bibliography. 12 illustrations. xiv + 266 pp. 5⅜ x 8.

20200-3 Paperbound $2.00

THE STYLES OF ORNAMENT, A. Speltz. The largest collection of line ornament in print, with 3750 numbered illustrations arranged chronologically from Egypt, Assyria, Greeks, Romans, Etruscans, through Medieval, Renaissance, 18th century, and Victorian. No permissions, no fees needed to use or reproduce illustrations. 400 plates with 3750 illustrations. Bibliography. Index. 640pp. 6 x 9. 20577-6 Paperbound $5.50

THE ART OF ETCHING, E. S. Lumsden. Every step of the etching process from essential materials to completed proof is carefully and clearly explained, with 24 annotated plates exemplifying every technique and approach discussed. The book also features a rich survey of the art, with 105 annotated plates by masters. Invaluable for beginner to advanced etcher. 374pp. 5⅜ x 8. 20049-3 Paperbound $3.75

OF THE JUST SHAPING OF LETTERS, Albrecht Dürer. This remarkable volume reveals Albrecht Dürer's rules for the geometric construction of Roman capitals and the formation of Gothic lower case and capital letters, complete with construction diagrams and directions. Of considerable practical interest to the contemporary illustrator, artist, and designer. Translated from the Latin text of the edition of 1535 by R. T. Nichol. Numerous letterform designs, construction diagrams, illustrations. iv + 43pp. 7⅛ x 10¾. 21306-4 Paperbound $2.00

DESIGN AND FIGURE CARVING, E. J. Tangerman. "Anyone who can peel a potato can carve," states the author, and in this unusual book he shows you how, covering every stage in detail from very simple exercises working up to museum-quality pieces. Terrific aid for hobbyists, arts and crafts counselors, teachers, those who wish to make reproductions for the commercial market. Appendix: How to Enlarge a Design. Brief bibliography. Index. 1298 figures. x + 289pp. 5⅜ x 8½.

21209-2 Paperbound $3.00

THE STANDARD BOOK OF QUILT MAKING AND COLLECTING, M. Ickis. Even if you are a beginner, you will soon find yourself quilting like an expert, by following these clearly drawn patterns, photographs, and step-by-step instructions. Learn how to plan the quilt, to select the pattern to harmonize with the design and color of the room, to choose materials. Over 40 full-size patterns. Index. 483 illustrations. One color plate. xi + 276pp. 6¾ x 9½.

20582-7 Paperbound $3.50

A HISTORY OF COSTUME, Carl Köhler. The most reliable and authentic account of the development of dress from ancient times through the 19th century. Based on actual pieces of clothing that have survived, using paintings, statues and other reproductions only where originals no longer exist. Hundreds of illustrations, including detailed patterns for many articles. Highly useful for theatre and movie directors, fashion designers, illustrators, teachers. Edited and augmented by Emma von Sichart. Translated by Alexander K. Dallas. 594 illustrations. 464pp. 5⅛ x 7⅛.

21030-8 Paperbound $4.00

Dover publishes books on commercial art, art history, crafts, design, art classics; also books on music, literature, science, mathematics, puzzles and entertainments, chess, engineering, biology, philosophy, psychology, languages, history, and other fields. For free circulars write to Dept. DA, Dover Publications, Inc., 180 Varick St., New York, N.Y. 10014.